HOW TO CUT COSTS IN BUSINESS

HOW TO
CUT
COSTS
IN BUSINESS

JOHN ALLAN

KOGAN
PAGE

First published in 1997

Apart from any fair dealing for the purposes of research or private study, or criticism or review, as permitted under the Copyright, Designs and Patents Act, 1988, this publication may only be reproduced, stored or transmitted, in any form or by any means, with the prior permission in writing of the publishers, or in the case of reprographic reproduction in accordance with the terms and licences issued by the CLA. Enquiries concerning reproduction outside those terms should be sent to the publishers at the undermentioned address:

Kogan Page Limited
120 Pentonville Road
London N1 9JN

© John Allan, 1997

The right of John Allan to be identified as author of this work has been asserted by him in accordance with the Copyright, Designs and Patents Act 1988.

British Library Cataloguing in Publication Data

A CIP record for this book is available from the British Library.

ISBN 0 7494 2070 7

Typeset by Saxon Graphics Ltd, Derby
Printed and bound in Great Britain by
Biddles Ltd, Guildford and King's Lynn

CONTENTS

INTRODUCTION

Most advice on cost cutting concentrates on sacking employees (euphemistically called 'downsizing') and bullying suppliers into lowering costs.

These are actually counter-productive. They may lower costs in the immediate future but have bad long-term effects. American studies show that companies that have downsized perform worse than those that have not. Japanese companies have found that partnerships with suppliers based on mutual trust and co-operation lead to lower costs and improved products, compared with normal confrontational Western methods.

In this book we will be looking at cutting labour costs and obtaining lower prices from suppliers, but this will not be the main focus. Instead we will be looking at all aspects of an organisation on the basis that an effectively run organisation has lower costs. This may take more time than a 'quick fix' of labour and purchase costs, but it will be longer lasting.

As you read through the book you will find that in several places you will need to produce and fill in a form to analyse your costs. This may seem time-consuming, but you will not be able to maximise cost cutting without analysis. You do not have to read through the book in sequence, but you will not maximise cost cutting unless you deal with all the areas covered.

If you are in manufacturing, you may wonder why there is not a chapter on this, your most important activity. It is not within the scope of a small book like this to address the complex questions of reducing manufacturing costs. These have been partly covered under the sections on finance, stockholding and process reengineering. When you have finished this book you should be able to apply the basic principles described to an analysis of your own production process. In particular you may find the concepts of process reengineering helpful.

In Chapter 8 there is a checklist to ensure that you have covered all the main areas for cost savings. At the end of the checklist is a section for you to add points that you want to action, as you read through the book. Whenever you come across a point for action, add it to the checklist.

References to organisations and books are incorporated in the main text for ease of use, or in the reference section at the end. Details were correct at the time of going to press but organisations may move or change their telephone number and books can go out of print! I considered that it was helpful to put in addresses and telephone numbers, even at the risk of change. The list is not meant to be complete, rather it is a list of starting points for your own investigation. The inclusion of an organisation does not imply that it is 'the best', simply that it is a good starting point.

My thanks to my wife Veronica, who reads every word that I write, for her invaluable advice, my researcher John Cadge and my expert reader Norman Maxfield.

My thanks also to you for buying this book. I welcome any comments – you will find the address for these at the end of Chapter 8 – a checklist for cost cutting.

ONE

PEOPLE

The management gurus used to recommend 'downsizing' to make organisations more competitive. This largely meant decreasing staffing to reduce costs and reducing the overall size of organisations to make them leaner and more efficient. This worked in the short term, but it is now realised that downsizing leads to loss of innovation and flexibility which are the lifeblood of any organisation. The short-term gains of downsizing have led to long-term disadvantages. Many organisations are now abandoning the concepts involved in downsizing.

The National Academy of Public Administration in the USA has a *Guide to Responsible Restructuring,* researched at the University of Colorado. It concludes that downsizing 'will produce little long term cost reduction; it may even increase costs'. Be warned! It advocates restructuring rather than cutting employee numbers. Dr Wayne Cascio at the University of Colorado, who carried out the studies, found that in a group of companies downsizing staff by 30%, at the end of three years total sales had only increased by 9% whilst other expenses increased by 11%. A control group of similar companies who had not downsized staff had sales increases of 26%! Cutting staff numbers is unlikely to benefit an organisation in the long term.

All too many organisations attempt to cut costs by wide-ranging decisions such as 'cut staff by 10% across the board' or 'no recruitment from outside for any post'. This is very short sighted and usually indicates that management has taken a panic decision without thinking through the process. Instead a goal should be set such as 'reduce staff costs by 10% without altering the efficiency and future development of the organisation'. This will take more time, and a lot of analysis, but will result in an organisation facing a future in which it can compete. Management should also first ask the question: 'Should costs be cut by reducing staffing costs or by some other means?'

As a rule, staff cuts should only be considered after all other avenues have been explored. Getting rid of staff may be a short-term gain but leads to long-term problems, especially when staff have to be recruited at a later stage. In particular the loss of experienced longer serving staff will lose your skills base and your company 'memory'. Staff cost cuts should be considered rather than staff number cuts.

Assuming that it is really necessary to reduce staff costs then you must carry out an audit. Two types of audit are required – structural and staff.

STRUCTURAL AUDIT (ONLY REQUIRED IN MEDIUM- AND LARGE-SIZED ORGANISATIONS)

This is really an audit that can only be taken at senior management level. The first question is: 'Do we have too many (or too few) levels of management?' There can be substantial advantages in reducing the number of levels to give a flatter organisational structure:

- It may be possible to reduce the total number of management staff, with resultant cost savings.
- The flattening of the structure by removing a layer of management will empower the next layer down by giving them the decision-making power of the layer that has been removed. This can lead to increased motivation and performance if handled correctly.
- Fewer layers of management can lead to quicker and better decision making.

It is possible (but usually very unlikely) that there needs to be an increase in the number of management levels. It is more likely that the basic structure of the organisation needs to change. Many organisations are going over to team structures – this will be discussed later on in this chapter.

The second question is: 'Is our structure the best structure for our organisation?' Many organisations are changing from a departmental structure to a team-based (or 'matrix') structure. Such structures can make considerable staff savings, whilst increasing efficiency and innovative ability.

In a team-based structure teams are set up for specific tasks. The teams cross normal departmental functions and team members are usually responsible to both their team leader and their departmental head.

Example:

Team	Dept 1	Dept 2	Dept 3	Dept 4	Dept 5
a	6	1	1	4	2
b					
c					

Departments are sales, production, accounts, etc.

Team 'a' is a customer liaison team responsible for getting orders, progressing production, invoicing, debt collection and after sales service. It has 14 members from sales, accounts, administration, servicing and production. The team leader is from sales. Members are responsible primarily to the team leader and secondarily to their department head. The accounts and administration members are also members for teams 'b' and 'c' acting as liaison. Team 'a' has responsibility for invoicing and debt collection, and the accounts department merely provides the mechanics for this. The accounts function could easily be carried out by outside contractors.

This is a complex but effective way of saving staff costs. Expert advice is needed before setting up a team/matrix company structure. Suitable specialist books on the subject are *How to Be a Better Teambuilder* by Rupert Eales-White and *Team Building: An Exercise in Leadership* by Robert B. Maddux. A section on teams follows later in this chapter.

STAFF AUDIT

Break the organisation down into departments (unless it is a very small organisation) and prepare a list of staff under job and skill categories. This will take some time, but is essential. In a large organisation, each department should submit its own audit.

Staff description	Number	Skills	Comment
Secretaries	9	Copy typing only	Easily recruited or trained in-house in 1 month
Secretaries	16	High. Use of WP plus spreadsheets. Knowledge of company culture plus methods	Require 3 months in-company training even if recruited as skilled

13

Staff description	Number	Skills	Comment
Filing juniors	7	Very basic	Easily recruited. Skills easily transferred to others

At the same time each department should produce a minimum staff skills requirement.

Staff description	Skills required	Minimum – ideal number
Secretaries	Copy typing	10–12
Secretaries	WP plus spreadsheet	10–12
Filing juniors	None	5–7

This example shows a minimum staff requirement of 25 and an ideal of 31. There is an extra member of staff over and above ideal levels at present. In theory seven staff could be shed, but clearly the excess is in the area of the skilled secretaries. They will be difficult to replace if extra staff are eventually needed.

At this stage each department needs to carry out a performance assessment for each staff member – in a simple format. It is to be hoped that there will be existing appraisals. If not, staff should be assessed under three simple categories.

Name	Excellent, capable of progress *	Good at present job	Poor, would prefer someone else
Fred Jones		✗	

* These will form the basis of your quality staff (see the section later in this chapter).

This final analysis will enable the decision on what should happen to each member of staff. Those with the worst performance should be asked to leave. Those with promotion potential may be able to be promoted if there is a shortage at the level above. Many organisations simply ask for voluntary redundancies. This usually results in the most skilled and experienced staff leaving as they will either have a high redundancy package or easily transferable skills. These are exactly the staff that you do not want to lose! Those that are left will be those who will find it difficult to get another job, with limited experience in the organisation. The management must choose those whom they wish to lose.

CUTTING STAFF

If staff costs have to be cut then the first target is costs rather than numbers. Cutting costs can entail altering jobs, using team structures, job sharing, incentive schemes, training and motivation. These can all cut staff costs without necessarily decreasing staff numbers. This will be dealt with later in this chapter.

If staff numbers have to be cut, then the audit of staff numbers, skills and performance forms the basis for deciding cuts. It is essential that staff cuts only affect areas where they can take place without affecting organisational performance. The audit may well have shown up essential areas requiring *more* staff. It will be as essential to ensure that the extra staff are provided for these areas, as to ensure that overall staff cuts are made. The concept of across the board staff cuts, or total freezes on all recruitment, can only be detrimental to organisational performance.

The first step after carrying out the audit is to identify those areas where it is *essential* that extra staff are provided. These will be areas where overall organisational performance is being held back by lack of staff. Extra staff need to be found from 'spare' staff in other areas, or outside recruitment.

The second step is to look at areas that are overstaffed, or where staff cuts can be made without affecting overall organisational performance. The audit will have indicated those areas that are overstaffed, and those individuals whose performance is below acceptable levels. The first action will be the dismissal of those staff who have unacceptable performance and are in overstaffed areas.

The third step is to look at those areas where there is no overstaffing, but there are staff whose performance is unsatisfactory. These staff should be dismissed and their place taken by existing staff from overstaffed departments whose performance is good.

This may seem a complicated approach but it has three purposes:

- To ensure that the organisation is not held back by lack of staff in key areas.
- To ensure that all retained staff are performing satisfactorily and that poor performers are replaced by satisfactory performers.
- To ensure that staff dismissed from areas that are overstaffed are not key performers.

After these three stages there may still be a requirement for a cut in staff numbers. This will inevitably mean that you are faced with dismissing staff who are performing satisfactorily. There is a temptation to keep the younger, lower-paid employees and dismiss older employees at higher rates of pay. If skill and experience are equal in both old and young, then this is sensible. In many cases dismissing older, more highly paid employees will remove your skills base and 'organisational memory'. In a year's time you may well wish that you had retained those with experience of events that only happen once every few years! It may be worth retaining older, higher-paid employees for this reason, and dismissing lower-paid employees.

When dismissing employees great care must be taken to comply with current legislation. Normally you will be in a redundancy situation since you will be cutting overall staffing numbers. The regulations and law in this area are complex, and regularly changing. If you have no personnel expert, you would be advised to get advice from an expert, or to consult your local Department of Employment. Leaflets are available – *Procedure for Handling Redundancies* and *Unfairly Dismissed?*

Where employees are being dismissed for unsatisfactory performance you will need to give the requisite warnings, both orally and in writing, before taking action. Beware, failure to conduct dismissals in the proper way can be costly!

Some employees may be nearing retirement and may be willing to take early retirement. Some employees may be willing to work part time instead of full time. These are also complicated areas where you will need to take advice.

The procedure for dismissals is too complicated to be discussed in this book, but it must be emphasised that failure to carry out the correct procedures can lead to expensive court or tribunal cases. Staff dismissal is not an easy option when it comes to cutting costs. Some companies employ most staff on short-term contracts, or casual working in order to facilitate dismissals. This may lead to easy dismissal but is unlikely to motivate staff to perform at maximum output!

CONTRACTING OUT

This is becoming a popular method of cutting staff costs. The process involves removing whole, or part, departments and replacing with services from outside. Common examples are:

- The replacement of a staff training department by external training agencies and consultants.

- The replacement of an accounting department by specialist external organisations for payroll, invoicing and payment functions.
- The replacement of a telephone switchboard and enquiry answering service by an external organisation which specialises in answering other people's telephones.
- The replacement of an advertising department by an external consultancy.
- The replacement of cleaners and maintenance staff by external contractors.
- The replacement of an information technology (IT) department by an external contractor – often another organisation with spare capacity.

There are many other examples. In many cases the cost savings can be considerable.

The opposite is also possible – renting out your services. You may be able to cut costs considerably, without dismissing staff, if you can sell their services to other organisations. Examples are:

- Where you have to maintain an IT department you may be able to take on IT work for another organisation, using your existing staff.
- You may be able to take on administrative and secretarial work to take up the slack in your staff utilisation (see Chapter 4 on Administration).
- You may be able to share a specialist member of staff with another organisation. For example, an emergency engineer could be shared between companies.

It is well worth considering whether you can dispense with departments and source the function externally, or whether you can rent out yourself. The calculations are, however, complex. You should ensure that you do not take a decision without professional advice.

Other methods of cutting staff costs

As an alternative or addition to cutting staff numbers, staff costs can be cut in the long term by improving the effectiveness of existing staff. This will enable expansion without increasing staff numbers and will allow natural wastage by staff leaving or retiring to reduce staff numbers without affecting efficiency. This will have the effect of reducing staff costs per unit of output – a useful cost saving! The main methods for improving efficiency are:

- recruiting quality staff only;

17

- altering jobs for better efficiency;
- using team structures;
- job sharing and part-time work;
- incentive schemes;
- training;

and perhaps most important of all

- motivation.

QUALITY STAFF

This may seem a strange heading for cost cutting but, since quality staff will perform better than normal staff, they will save costs. Quality staff are those who do not just do a job competently – they *excel.* They produce higher quality work in a shorter time than normal staff. They are highly motivated to perform for you. Employing only quality staff takes time and effort, but it is well worth while. If you have carried out a staff audit as detailed above, then you have the basis for a start on a quality staff programme. You can obtain quality staff in two ways:

- Only recruit quality staff when recruiting. Do *not* recruit someone who is not quality. If you cannot find someone who is quality, then start the process again to find more candidates. Taking on non-quality staff only builds up long-term problems and increases costs. Do not accept second best! If necessary use temporary staff or temporary arrangements until you have found the right person.
- If you have staff who have the potential to become quality staff, then spend time training and motivating them to perform. Transformation of normal staff to quality staff will cut costs and pay for the process very quickly. There are sections on training and motivating later in this chapter. You will be able to identify staff who can become quality staff if you have a system of regular appraisal. Suitable books on the subject are *Effective Performance Appraisals* by Robert B. Maddux, *Performance Appraisals* by Martin Fisher and *Appraising Your Staff* by Philip Moon (forthcoming).

The cost of hiring quality staff is usually little different from normal staff. Quality staff derive great satisfaction from performing well. They are motivated primarily by job satisfaction rather than income.

Is the job right?

It is no use having the right quality people if your jobs are not properly structured. At the start of this chapter we saw that restructuring was more likely to save money than staff cuts. Structuring jobs correctly is the first part of restructuring an organisation.

Before restructuring a job it is first necessary to write a job description. This is a description of what the job should be ideally, rather than what it is at present. After the job description has been produced it needs to be examined on the following basis:

- Is the job, as described, suitable for the organisation in the future? If not, what changes need to be made?
- Would the job fully occupy one person? Is there a possibility of adding to it and enlarging the job?
- Is there any way in which the job can be made more interesting? Quality staff work best at interesting jobs. Boredom leads to low output and increased costs.

Through restructuring jobs you will often find that ten jobs can be reduced to nine, cutting costs and at the same time adding to job interest. Care must be taken not to overload staff in the process.

Using teams

Earlier on in this chapter we looked at the concept of team structures. A team structure for a company is usually only sensible for medium- to large-sized companies. Small companies can work as a team without the need for a formal team structure.

Advantages of teams are:

- Teams cut across demarcation lines. A task is carried out by the team as a whole and not by individuals carrying out their narrow functions. This usually means that a team tackling a task will be smaller than the number of individuals needed to deal with the task under the normal departmental structure.
- Teams do not become locked in to systems and structures. They are flexible and usually carry out tasks more quickly than a group of individuals under a departmental structure.
- Team members get more job satisfaction than individuals working on their own. This leads to high motivation and high performance.
- Team structure normally requires fewer senior managers for control than normal departmental structures.

- Once staff have been trained as team members they can easily switch between teams as required, giving greater labour flexibility and savings in overall staff costs.

Part time/job sharing

The use of part-time working and job sharing instead of full-time working can reduce costs. It can also allow use of mothers who wish to devote only part of a day to work. There is also an increasing tendency for those over 40, particularly those who have been made redundant, to take several part-time jobs rather than a full-time one. The reasons for this are complex but are primarily that a number of part-time jobs are often easier to obtain than a full-time one, and a spread of part-time jobs gives more security as you are unlikely to lose them all at once!

This means that there is, at present, a pool of those who would prefer part-time work or job sharing.

Part-time work is best kept to under 12 hours a week to avoid paying National Insurance. The rules vary with circumstances – check with your local Department of Employment. Part-time work is best suited to jobs where a full-time member of staff is not required. For example, cleaners may only be required for four hours a day, post room staff may only be needed between 7 am and 10 am and then 3 pm to 6 pm.

As a rule, job sharing means the sharing of one full-time job between two or more people. This is increasingly seen by companies as an attractive option because:

- Two (or more) people are more flexible than one person. At times of high workload they may be able to overlap and work together, whilst at times of low workload they may be able to cut down on hours.
- If one is off ill then the other can usually cover to some extent.
- Two people may be able to bring more skills to a task than a single individual.
- If the people involved work less than 12 hours, then the costs to the company are normally lower than those of a full-time employee.
- Job sharing may enable a company to keep a valued employee who can only work part time, in a job that the company needs to be full time.

Overall, part-time working and job sharing offer a company flexibility and lower costs. It is worth looking carefully at all current jobs to see whether part-time working and job sharing can be introduced. In addition, each time a job needs to be filled, part-time working or job sharing should be carefully considered.

INCENTIVE SCHEMES

Incentive schemes are often used to increase production per member of staff and thus cut costs. A good scheme can be excellent in cutting costs, but bad schemes can severely damage output. Not all incentive schemes work! To be successful an incentive scheme needs to be:

- Easy to install.
- Easily understood by the staff involved.
- Recognised as fair.
- Have a result which is easily measured and understood.
- Able to increase output or cut costs.
- Cheat-proof!
- Give a reward now rather than later.

Incentive scheme rewards do not need to be financial. Some companies have a Porsche which the best salesperson in each month is given for a month's use. For many people the Porsche in the drive and recognition as the best salesperson count for more than money!

For an incentive scheme to work it needs to have easily defined goals which are measurable and understood. The reward for achievement does not have to be great, it has to be recognised. This is why many companies reward achievement by putting up a photograph of the achiever. To have your photograph in the lobby of a hotel as 'employee of the month' can be a great incentive.

Before starting a financial incentive scheme, you should consider whether a non-financial scheme is possible. You may be able to improve performance and cut costs without a great deal of financial expense. The awarding of a small prize in public by one of the directors with a great deal of praise may count for a lot. You should try this first. As a start on incentive schemes why not announce a prize for the best suggestion for cutting costs? You may be surprised at the quality of the suggestions; the staff on the ground are more likely to know where costs can be cut than senior management!

TRAINING

For quite some time now, many British companies have seen training as an expense to be avoided if at all possible. Often training departments have been cut out, and all training carried out by consultants and training agencies. Training has been kept to a minimum covering only essential areas. In the very short term this may save money. In the long term it results in a poorly trained workforce, untrained in the latest techniques and performing below maximum. This will not save money, it will cost money as the result of inefficiencies.

Training can help you cut costs for the following reasons:

- Trained staff are more efficient and have a higher output than untrained staff.
- Trained staff have fewer accidents, and accidents are costly.
- Trained staff have higher quality output and fewer rejects.
- Trained staff get it right first time.
- Trained staff are more likely to be motivated and happy.
- Trained staff can use the latest methods and equipment which are usually cheaper.

In order to be cost effective training must be carefully targeted. Unnecessary training wastes rather than saves money.

In order to target training correctly, a training survey should be carried out. This looks at each area of operation and determines the benefits of training on a cost-effectiveness basis. It is useful to use a form similar to the one below.

Department/ job	Training possible	Training cost	Likely cost savings
Switchboard	1-day course for filing clerk to be trained as relief switchboard operative	£240	No need to recruit new switchboard operative. Difference in salary between clerk and operative £1000 pa
Widget operatives	On-the-job training to enable minor machine adjustments to be made by operative rather than engineer	£150 in downtime – estimated	£500 pa in not having to wait for engineer

Although it will take some time, this exercise will more than pay for itself in cost savings. Normally only training that can result in cost savings should be implemented. There may, of course, be reasons for training which has no short-term cost benefit. An example would be training to develop someone who has long-term potential for promotion.

It is not always possible to quantify savings, for example in areas of safety. Areas such as this should be classed as 'essential' even though there is no obvious cost saving. In reality the cost saving is the cost of a serious accident. Although this may be covered by insurance to some extent, the hidden costs of an accident can be very high.

In many cases training should be considered at the same time as new equipment purchases. The cost of new equipment may also include relevant training. The cost of both equipment and training needs to be considered to see if the purchase will be cost effective.

MOTIVATION

You are more likely to cut costs in the long term by motivating people to perform to the maximum than you are from shedding staff.

Well-motivated staff have the following advantages:

- Motivated staff will normally produce more.
- Motivated staff are less likely to leave (and cause costs for taking on new staff).
- Motivated staff are likely to take less sick leave.
- Motivated staff have less quality rejections.
- Motivated staff will respond better to the needs of your customers.

You will notice similarities to the list under 'Training'. Training is a good method of motivating staff.

How can staff be motivated? This is really an area for a specialist book (*How to Be Better at Motivating People* by John Allan) but the essentials are:

Assuming that pay and working conditions are acceptable (they do not need to be exceptional) most employees:

- Need to feel that their work is worth while.
- Need to see the end results of their work.
- Need social contact with others.
- Need to feel personal achievement.
- Need to feel that they have some control over their work
- Most of all – need praise.

None of these need incur costs but they produce motivated employees who will cut costs. Motivation is a very cost-effective way of making cost savings! Some of these 'needs' can be met by a suitable incentive scheme, especially a well-designed non-financial one (see above). Some simple ways of meeting these needs and motivating your staff are:

Give praise. Praise costs nothing yet many people are very reluctant to give it! Public praise is even more effective than private praise. Praise can also be used as a method of correction which is acceptable to the employee:

> I really like the quality of the widgets that you produce, Sheila, but we need to produce more each hour if we are going to get the order out in time.

Praise given at the same time as the request for a higher output is more likely to produce results than pure criticism such as:

> Your output is not high enough, Sheila, you must produce more if we are going to get the order out on time.

Enable people to feel achievement. This can be done through suitable training, through setting targets and giving praise for making target, through making people feel that their efforts are worth while.

Social contact can be provided in many ways. At the work place it may be possible to arrange matters so that people can easily talk (although talking must not be allowed to act as a distraction). A communal place where people can eat will also provide a suitable place for social contact. Outings for work groups and newsletters can also help.

Making people feel that their *work is worth while* can often be achieved by showing them the *end result of their work*. Many employees only know about the small operation that they carry out, they are unaware of the end product or service. Enabling them to see the end product or service puts their own work in context and enables them to feel that their work is worth while. This may be quite difficult but the motivational effect is considerable.

Allowing employees to have *some control over their job* may be as simple as allowing some discretion on the way in which the job is done, or the order in which the various tasks can be carried out. At the other end of the scale there has been considerable success with the concept of teams having total responsibility for a task, but being allowed to determine how they carry it out. They could be given cutting the cost as part of the task. In Japan such teams have made considerable cost savings.

SUMMARY

People are valuable, you may not always benefit from reducing their numbers. If you have to reduce numbers, keep the best!

If you are reducing staff costs consider buying in services and altering the way in which people work to give maximum efficiency.

Quality staff will cut your costs! Think carefully about how you can motivate and train them, and how you can organise them to best advantage.

A proper evaluation of your staffing combined with an approach that enables you to motivate your employees to maximum performance will lead to considerable cost savings. Initial cost savings will result from your adjustment of staffing levels, the long-term savings will flow from motivation and training.

TWO

PURCHASING

Purchasing is one of the most obvious ways of cutting costs. If you can reduce the cost of your purchases, or use the way you purchase to reduce other costs, you can often produce substantial cost cuts. The way in which you purchase is crucial to your organisation's profitability. Too often purchasing is left to someone who is unskilled. They will often be purchasing from professionals who are highly trained to obtain the highest possible price for their goods or service! Are you sending out an amateur to play with the professionals?

GOLDEN RULE NO 1 ALWAYS FIELD A SKILLED, PREPARED, PURCHASER

This does not necessarily mean someone with years of experience and a qualification. It means someone who, at least, understands the principles of purchasing and has done their homework on the purchase to be made. This chapter will explain some of the basic principles involved in good purchasing.

There are two other Golden Rules. They concern the person doing the purchasing. After 20 years of purchasing (or buying as it is called in retailing) I am certain that they are indeed Golden Rules.

GOLDEN RULE NO 2 NEVER BLUFF

This may seem a strange rule; many people believe that a purchaser needs to bully and bluff to get the best price. This is not so! The one certainty of bluffing is that you will eventually be found out. When this happens your suppliers will see you as a bluffer and tend to ignore your threats. The one time when you really mean it, they will assume you are bluffing which could have serious consequences. It always pays to make statements that are true, although this does not mean that you have to disclose everything when you make a statement.

GOLDEN RULE NO 3 BE FAIR

In the Far East the only successful negotiations are those where neither side loses out. They believe that only if neither side loses out will the agreement be kept and further business arise. All too often in the West we think it is necessary in negotiations to have a winner and a loser. A deal that is fair to both sides will be carried through willingly by both sides and a relationship will have been built up that can lead to long-term mutually beneficial business. However, being fair does not mean that you cannot be tough. The ideal negotiation is one where both sides have argued their case strongly, a great deal of haggling has taken place and an agreement eventually struck where both sides comment: 'That was tough, I had to give a bit away, but in the end the deal is acceptable.'

HOW TO NEGOTIATE LOW PRICES

To which we need to add 'without bluffing and by being fair'! The first step is to research your supplier. Your supplier will almost certainly have researched you! The second step is to consider the alternatives. The third step is to work out your stance for negotiations. The fourth step is to negotiate and close the deal.

Very few companies regularly review their purchasing. Most tend to stay with an acceptable supplier and continue buying without further negotiations. At the very least you should have an annual review of your suppliers to ensure that prices are keen and service satisfactory. You will, therefore, have two reasons for negotiating a price. One is that you have a new supplier or a new product/service. The other is that you are reviewing a supplier, product or service and decide to negotiate a better price. Even with a valued existing supplier there is no reason why you cannot explain that you are carrying out your annual review of prices - check the prices from other sources and if necessary renegotiate with the existing supplier. Many people get annual quotes from several sources every year for their private car insurance. Why should a business be any less vigilant?

Researching your supplier

1. How do you rate as a customer?

How important are you to the supplier? Are you a major purchaser or a small purchaser? What is your record for paying bills? Is your order quantity economic? Are your delivery requirements going to cause problems? A supplier is likely to tailor prices according to your importance to him or her. If you are an important customer, then this puts you in a strong position for negotiating price.

If you think you are an important customer, then it is always worth asking what percentage of your supplier's sales you represent. If your supplier is unwilling to tell you, and is a limited company, you can work this out yourself by looking at the turnover in the last published accounts. You can do this through credit agencies such as Dun and Bradstreet, Holmer Farm Way, High Wycombe, Bucks, Tel: 01494 422000 for a small charge. As a rule of thumb if you account for 10% of a company's sales, then you are in a strong position. It is worth considering whether you could cut down on the number of your suppliers, give some more business and thus be a more important customer. This would also cut down on your administration costs.

A supplier also values a customer who pays on time, causes little trouble and is pleasant! A customer who does not pay on time, complains a lot and is unpleasant will, all other things being equal, find it more difficult to get a lower price. We are all human! You should aim to become a valued customer and then use this position as a leverage for better prices.

You could also announce that you are producing a 'preferred supplier' list, and will only be dealing with companies on this list. Many will try very hard to get on it!

2. How badly do they need the business?

If your supplier needs the business badly, then you are in a strong position. There are several indicators for this.

- How desperate is the representative? If he or she seems overkeen to sell, or is very willing to discuss price, then it could indicate a real need to sell. The need may be the company's, or the representative's to make target, it does not matter which.
- Is the company making slim profits or a loss? You can find this out from published figures or from a credit agency. Low profits or dropping sales will again give you an indication that a company will be keen to sell to you.

- Has there been a lot of new competition? If several new companies have appeared on the scene offering the same products, your supplier will be trying to stop them poaching business.
- Have any of your supplier's major customers gone out of business, had a large drop in sales or started using another supplier? Your supplier will be keen to replace the lost business.
- Has there been a recent change in management, particularly the sales management, or a change in representative. New people will want to make a quick impression with increased sales.
- Is there likely to be a cash flow problem? They may offer a discount for quick payment.

If your supplier needs your business badly, then you are in a strong position to negotiate lower prices. You may find it best to offer a larger order or combine several regular small orders into one big one. The lower price may well cover the extra costs of buying in a larger quantity.

3. What deals are available at the start of negotiations?

Always find out the best deal on offer before you start negotiations. If you do not find this out, then your hard negotiations may only get you the normal 'best price'. You must find out the best price before offering anything on your side. Keep larger quantities, earlier payment and any other incentive up your sleeve for the real negotiations. Never assume that the list price is the best price. Always ask what the best price is, you will be surprised at how often there is one.

4. Who will you negotiate with?

The secret here is only to negotiate with the person who can make the decision. If representatives cannot make the decision on price and have to refer the decision back to head office, then you are wasting your time negotiating with them. Referring the price back gives them an advantage of thinking time. Always ask whether the person you are talking to has authority to make the price decision. If not, then insist on talking to the person who can. This assumes, of course, that you are authorised to take the decision on your side.

The opposite side of this tactic (assuming you are not the boss!) is, when faced with a refusal to go to a lower price, to say that you are not authorised to pay such a high price and will have to refer the decision upwards. This gives you thinking time and places the supplier at a disadvantage.

What are the strengths and weaknesses of the person with whom you are negotiating? Try and write them down. You will need to avoid situations where they can use their strengths, and try and create situations where their weaknesses will be exposed. As an example, if someone is very expert on the product then do not allow technical specification to become an important part of the negotiation. If they are weak on the technicalities of the product then ask a lot of detailed technical questions and express surprise that they cannot answer them fully! The intention is to put yourself, not them, in control of the negotiations.

What are the alternatives?

If you have an alternative to buying from the supplier, then you are in a strong position. If you do not like the price, then you can refuse the deal. Equally, if you have to buy the product or service from the supplier (if, for example, they are the only suppliers), then you are in a weak position. Before a negotiation it pays to consider whether there are alternatives.

1. Use an alternative supplier

In many cases there are alternative suppliers. In office stationery and cleaning services, for example, there will be several alternative suppliers. If you do not like the price, then you can go elsewhere. You must check the price at alternative suppliers; they could be higher and your existing supplier turn out to be best! Before a negotiation always check out prices at alternative suppliers and aim to better them in your negotiation. This 'shopping around' is essential. You should never buy without knowing the market price of the product or service.

2. Do not buy now

If you can wait for your purchase, then you are in a strong position. If the price does not suit, then you can reject the deal. You are in an especially strong position if the supplier is keen to sell now. You will only agree to buy now if the price is right. Buying at the month end can also be effective as it may give you the maximum credit period if the processing by the supplier's invoice department has just been done.

3. Give them something

An alternative to a normal deal might be one where in return for a better price you give the supplier something. This might be quicker payment, a larger order quantity, a chance to carry out a service at a time most convenient to the supplier. Your aim is to make a deal for a lower price in return for your co-operation. In some cases you might agree to buy an additional product or service; many suppliers have 'linked' deals for purchases of several products.

The negotiation

You have done your research on your supplier. You have considered all the alternatives - now comes the crunch; the negotiation.

1. Deciding on what your limits are

Before starting any negotiation it is essential to work out your ideal, acceptable and bottom line prices. The ideal price is the very lowest price that you can sensibly expect. You have done your homework and know how keen (or otherwise) the supplier is to sell. The ideal price is the very lowest price he or she will be likely to go to. The acceptable price will be a little above this, but still a good price. You will be happy to pay this. The bottom line price is the very highest price that you are prepared to pay. Higher than this and you do not buy. This may not be the list price. You may have found an alternative supplier and your bottom line price is the one you can obtain from them.

In negotiations you will bargain strongly to get your ideal price, but will be prepared to move towards your acceptable price if you have to. You will strongly resist moving up to your bottom line price unless you absolutely have to. Just setting these simple, price points makes a great difference to your negotiation. You know exactly where you are and how strongly you have to make your case.

2. Treating the supplier correctly

Do not keep your supplier waiting. It is discourteous and will be annoying. I have been on the selling side as well as the buying side, and I can assure you that being kept waiting is annoying and makes a price reduction *less* likely! If you cannot see your supplier straight away, make sure a cup of tea or coffee is offered and an apology given. This ensures that the supplier has positive feelings towards you when negotiations start.

3. When not to negotiate

Do not get into a negotiation if you are tired, in a hurry, angry, under pressure or have had a few drinks. In other words do not negotiate when you are not at your best. Postpone to another day. Better a postponement than a bad negotiation.

4. Win-win

The ideal of all negotiations. Both sides leave feeling that they have won. More commonly both sides leave feeling that they have not lost! If your suppliers leave feeling that they have lost, you will only have won if you never need to do business with them again. They may do everything possible to ensure that you get minimum benefit from the deal.

If your purchase is the only one that you will ever make from a supplier, and the product or service is so tightly defined that you can check exactly what you get, then go for the kill. Negotiate the lowest price you can get. If you are going to make regular purchases, then it is in your long-term interests to ensure that the supplier leaves the meeting without feeling that they have lost. A happy long-term relationship with a supplier is beneficial. If you have a good relationship, then the one time when you really need a low price or a quick delivery, the supplier will try and help.

Of course win-win does not mean that you do not have tough negotiations. It means leaving the other party with some self-respect. If you have negotiated a very low price, for example, you can commiserate and say 'it's a shame prices have to be so low, it's a tough market'. The supplier can then leave feeling it was not his or her fault, it was market forces at work. It is all part of being fair to suppliers and maintaining good relationships. In the long run it pays off.

5. Tying down the deal

You have done your preparation, considered all the alternatives and then carried out a tough negotiation. What many people then forget to do is to close the deal in a way that ensures it happens. At the end of your negotiations repeat the details of the deal and state that you will confirm them in writing (unless the deal is a very small one). It is surprising how often people have different memories of a deal! Unless you confirm in writing there is a chance that a disagreement about what exactly was agreed may occur. Your supplier may want to confirm the details, in which case write down your understanding of what was agreed and check your supplier's confirmation carefully.

If your supplier is confirming the details, read the agreement throughout, including the small print, on receipt. Write to your supplier immediately if you find something with which you disagree. If you do not point out any disagreement immediately, your supplier will assume that you agree the confirmation.

CHEAPEST MAY NOT ALWAYS BE BEST! (BUT IT OFTEN IS)

There is no good reason for always accepting the cheapest quote. Many people do not accept the cheapest quote for a house extension because they are unhappy with the reputation of the builder or find a more expensive quote more closely matches their requirements. The same is true when purchasing for a company. Before accepting any quotation you should consider:

- Am I happy with the company quoting? What is its reputation?
- Is the product or service of suitable quality for me?
- Are the delivery times and conditions acceptable?
- Are the payment terms acceptable?
- Do I feel entirely happy about the deal?

If you are not happy, do not buy.

At home I often pay a little more to buy from a local supplier who I know personally and who I can insist sorts out any problems. In a small business it may make sense to pay a little more for freedom from trouble. Your time is valuable, it costs money when you sort out problems. You have to set off the possible problems against the likely savings. It is worth writing down a list of problems and savings, and looking at it carefully. Only buy cheaply if the problems are unlikely or are outweighed by cost savings.

On the other hand a cheaper product or service may be sensible even if the quality is lower than you have had previously if for example:

- The quality is still acceptable.
- The credit terms are better.
- Deliveries are in a form that enable you to make savings.

We will look at these one by one.

1. Quality

It may make sense to cut costs by buying lower quality if that lower quality does not affect the goods or services that you produce. It may even make sense if the rejection rate of your product goes up as long as the cost savings justify this. It almost never makes sense if your customers' rejection rate of your product goes up. A potato chip manufacturer could buy perfect potatoes with no blemishes. These would make perfect chips, but they would be expensive. Instead the chip manufacturer may buy relatively low-quality potatoes. The chips with blemishes or faults are rejected by an optical sorting machine leaving only perfect chips. The reject chips are turned into mashed potato for other products. The low cost of imperfect potatoes normally far outweighs the loss from turning reject chips into mash.

2. Credit terms

You may well find that a supplier is offering better credit terms for the product or service that you want. If you are at present paying in 30 days, you may well find a supplier who is prepared to allow you 90 days. The extra 60 days are worth money to you, and have to be balanced against any reduction in quality. This will be discussed fully later under 'Specifying to cut costs'.

3. Delivery arrangements

You may be able to get a cheaper price by rearranging deliveries. If you are ordering once a month then you may be able to arrange weekly delivery. This would ease stock levels and, if you pay on invoice, cash flow. Similarly, if you buy weekly at present you might negotiate a better price for a monthly delivery.

These cost savings have to be balanced against any reduction in quality. You will have to carry out an analysis:

- Is the reduction in quality going to have any effect on what we do in terms of providing a product or service?
- If there is an effect, will it be noticeable to the customer or will it result in increased costs for our service or product?
- Will any increased costs be more than offset by the savings that we make in purchasing?

Only after a detailed analysis should you be willing to accept a quality reduction.

CREDIT WHERE CREDIT IS DUE!

You may well be able to get your credit extended. Often a discount is given for prompt payment, ie 2% for payment within 28 days. This may well be just a method of ensuring that payment is made within 28 days and no extension may be possible. On the other hand it may be possible to pay in 90 days and forgo the 2%. This may well be worth while if it helps your cash flow. It does not hurt to ask what terms are available and if you are unhappy – negotiate! Do not, however, just decide to pay in 90 days instead of 28 days without discussing it. If word gets round that you are a bad payer you may find companies unwilling to supply you, or increasing prices to cover bad debt risk.

You may also be able to negotiate an extension of credit in exchange for a reduced discount, a credit charge or a higher product price. It is sometimes possible to pay with a series of post-dated cheques. All of these methods have to be set against the benefit in cash flow and credit cost. If you have a cash flow problem or have a bank overdraft with a high interest rate, then it may well make sense to pay for extended credit. You will have to calculate whether it is worth while.

Your supplier may have cash flow problems. They may be very willing to buy early payment from you. One company that I know offers to pay in seven days (instead of 30–40 days) in return for a 2% discount. Many small suppliers take up the offer as it helps their cash flow and the company has had its cost prices reduced by 2%. This is worth while because the company concerned has a positive cash flow with money in the bank earning an interest rate far less than 2% per seven days. If you have money in the bank then consider paying early for a discount. You may also get a discount for paying by direct debit.

You can reduce your purchase price if you can renegotiate payment terms. A saving of only 1% through renegotiated payment terms can make a substantial contribution to your bottom line profits. It pays to ask for better terms!

ALTERNATIVE SUPPLIERS

Finding them

It is very rare to have only one possible supplier for a purchase. Even gas, telephone and electricity come with alternative suppliers nowadays. If you are big enough you could even find alternative water suppliers. For most purchases you will have a choice, but for how many of your purchases have you really investigated the possibility of alternative supply? Alternative suppliers will often yield cost savings in excess of 10%, well worth the effort of finding them!

How do you find alternative suppliers? It is often quite difficult, especially with a specialist supplier. You will almost certainly have to invest a little money and some time. Here are some suggestions:

1. The next time the representative calls ask him/her why they are better than their main competitors. This will almost certainly mean that they will have to tell you who their main competitors are. It will also alert them to the fact that you are considering alternatives and may sharpen their prices!

2. Invest in a CD-ROM of *Yellow Pages* (if you have a CD-ROM on your computer). This will enable you to do a national search for suppliers. If you do not have a CD-ROM then invest in *Yellow Pages* for several areas around you. You can also phone the Talking Pages service of *Yellow Pages* and get a free national search.
3. Find out if there is a trade directory covering the area of supply. Most trades have a suitable directory listing all suppliers. There are also general directories such as *Kelly's*.
4. Ask another company near you (but not a competitor!) whether they have found any alternative suppliers.
5. For overseas supplies contact the trade department at the embassies of countries who could supply and ask for a list of suitable suppliers.

These are only some suggestions. You might be able to arrange for a trainee or office junior to do the basic research for you. A few days finding alternative suppliers for all your main purchases, and making initial contact, would be a small price to pay against the possible savings.

Draw up a list of possible suppliers. Phone each one to check that they do supply the product or service that you want and that they are able to supply you.

Comparing suppliers

When you have a list of possible suppliers, you need to compare them with each other and your existing supplier. To do this you need to produce a chart. A suitable one would be:

Comparison of suppliers					
	Supplier a	Supplier b	Supplier c	Supplier d	Supplier e
Product					
Product quality					
Price					
Terms					
Delivery					
People					

Once you have filled in the details, it will be easier to compare the suppliers. Initially you will probably only have checked that the supplier can provide the product/service that you require. You will now have to check price and terms. Eliminate any suppliers where the price and terms are much worse than your existing supplier.

You will now be left with a list of possible suppliers where the product is available, and initial discussions on price and terms indicate that they are suitable for evaluation. You should try and make this list no greater than about five companies.

You will need further discussions with each of these suppliers either by telephone, or by means of a visit by their representative. This will enable you to check quality, discuss delivery arrangements, negotiate best price and terms and make a judgement on the people that you will deal with. Many companies ignore the 'people' aspect, but it is very important. There is not much point in dealing with someone that you do not like and cannot trust – even if the price is low!

When discussing price it is usually a good idea to make it clear that there are other suppliers competing for the business. You should certainly make this clear to your existing supplier as a matter of courtesy. The knowledge that others are competing for the business usually sharpens prices.

At the end of the process you will have to make a decision on which supplier to use based on your analysis. It may be possible to try out a new supplier whilst still temporarily continuing with the old one. This is the ideal situation. It may also be possible to use two suppliers at the same time. If you are not compromised on price or delivery because of this, it will be very useful to ensure dual supply in case of problems.

SPECIFYING TO CUT COSTS

It is often possible to cut costs by respecifying the product/service ordered. The product/service may be overspecified, or an alternative satisfactory specification may be cheaper.

In order to ensure the cheapest specification ask the following questions:

- Have I asked the supplier if there is an alternative cheaper specification that fits the bill?
- Could I alter the quality to obtain a cheaper price?
- Could I alter the process that I use the product/service for to enable me to order a cheaper specification?

An alternative specification may be cheaper and still perfectly suited to your purpose. As an example many organisations have daily cleaning when weekly may be satisfactory or may order 90 gsm paper for their copier when 75 gsm is satisfactory. Often specifications are out of date and have not been examined for several years.

Quality can often be safely downgraded. Many cars are filled with normal four-star petrol when they can safely take unleaded at a lower price. Even if your reject rate rises slightly, it may still make sense to downgrade if the cost savings more than justify the rejects. Often your product/service quality is higher than your customer really requires. By downgrading your purchases you may be able to offer an acceptable product and a lower price, and still make extra profit through cost savings. Are you ordering too high a quality or offering too high a quality? If so, you are throwing money away.

Processes can often be altered to allow for a cheaper specification. Paper can be made from wood pulp, rags and even certain types of grass such as esparto grass. Could you alter your process or service so that you could specify a cheaper ingredient?

You can often specify different timing for delivery of a product/service to cut costs. You may normally specify delivery on a Monday which means a special trip for the supplier. By ordering on a Thursday when he or she is already in your area, you may be able to negotiate a lower cost. It is always worth asking whether a different day makes a difference. Many companies offer a 'next day' service for their product which means first-class post or special delivery service. By asking for a slower service you may save money on carriage costs.

MAKE YOUR SUPPLIER DO THE WORK

Are there things that your supplier can do better than you? A company that I know spent a long time weighing out small quantities of expensive ingredients. Mistakes in weighing often affected their product badly. Eventually they got their supplier to supply the ingredients in pre-weighed bags of the correct weights. They saved a great deal of time and had a more consistent product. The supplier only made a small charge for the service, far less than their labour costs had been in weighing. They saved money by getting their supplier to carry out part of their process and improved their product at the same time.

Could your supplier:

- Carry out part of your process?
- Prepare the product for your process?

- Supply in quantity or format that suits your process better?
- Help you modify your process to better use their product/service?

Consider your supplier as part of your process and integrate them into it.

JUST IN TIME

One of the greatest revolutions in purchasing in recent years has been 'just in time' (JIT) ordering. This is discussed further in Chapter 3. It was one of the factors that gave the Japanese a competitive edge in the motor industry. In essence it simply means getting product/service delivered at the time when it is required – no earlier, no later. This means that stock-holding can be cut substantially with a saving in costs. Of course you need a supplier that you can totally rely on to deliver on time!

A large company using JIT will plan production weeks ahead and advise every supplier exactly what product is required at what time. A complex computer program dovetails ordering with production and suppliers face penalties if they deliver late. A small company can still make use of this technique if it is prepared to spend some staff time in order to save money.

SUMMARY

Time spent in examining purchase decisions in detail will almost always result in action which can cut costs. The cost of goods and services that you buy significantly affects your profit and viability.

It is best to achieve lower costs through co-operation from suppliers. A good relationship with suppliers is the best foundation for sound purchasing.

You should carry out regular purchasing reviews, identifying your most important purchases and ensuring that you are buying these at the right price by an analysis of the item purchased, and the alternative suppliers for it.

What can your supplier do for you? You may be able to shift some of your work load on to your supplier at little cost.

Always prepare for negotiations; the time spent on this will always pay off. Never assume that the quoted prices or terms are unalterable, you can usually do better.

THREE
FINANCE AND STOCKS

THE CONTROL OF YOUR WORKING CAPITAL

Many organisations only look at purchase and staff costs when they consider cutting costs. Finance can, however, be one of the best areas for cost cutting. It is also usually an area where cost cutting does not mean performance cutting. The same applies to stockholdings where cutting stock levels can often lead to improved quality and performance.

In considering cost cutting in finance and stocks we will look at the following areas:

- The cost of banking.
- The cost of finance and alternative sources of finance (including shareholders).
- Overdrafts versus loans.
- Leasing and renting rather than buying.
- Stock control.
- Debtor control.
- Creditor control.
- Budgets and cash flow as a cost cutting tool.

COST OF BANKING

The cost of banking is not fixed. Bank managers have some discretion over the way that charges are calculated.

- Find out how your charges are being calculated. For smaller organisations the charge is usually based on the 'activity' in the account and usually by means of a fixed charge per transaction. Large organisations sometimes have a fixed percentage of the turnover of the account. Negotiate with your bank manager for whichever is cheapest.

- Ask about computerised services such as BACS (Bankers Automated Clearing Services). You may be able to pay your suppliers electronically and your customers may be able to pay you electronically. If you set up such a system you may be able to combine it with a system for placing and receiving orders electronically – saving more money.
- Minimise your overdraft by banking cheques and money daily – unless the amounts are very small in which case the transaction charge will probably mean that you should only bank once a week.
- Check your statements regularly. Banks do make mistakes.
- Produce a regular cash flow statement (see later in this chapter) to enable you to minimise overdraft charges.

COST AND SOURCES OF FINANCE

Each source of finance has different associated costs. The main sources are:

- High Street banks.
- Central schemes.
- Financial companies.
- Venture capital companies.
- Investment companies.
- Shareholders.
- 'Angels'.

Very considerable savings can be made by choosing the right source of finance. The savings could mean the difference between profit and loss for your organisation!

High Street banks

These are usually the first port of call for smaller companies. After all they normally have an account with a High Street bank, the bank manager knows them and loans or overdrafts seem reasonably simple to arrange.

The problem is that few High Street bank managers have any authority to give business loans or sizeable overdrafts. Most High Street banks have a system where business loans and overdrafts are approved by an area or central office with most of the evaluation of the proposal being done by a computer! If you have conducted your business for several years, have never gone over your overdraft limit and have an exemplary balance sheet, then the bank will be willing to give you a loan. If you are in this enviable situation then you probably do not need a loan or extended overdraft, and it is when you are not in this situation that you do need one!

An added problem is that many High Street banks also review their overdrafts by computer and you could suddenly find that your overdraft limit is reduced because the computer program no longer rates you a good risk. Unlikely? Well, it has recently happened to a small company of which I am a director. The bank's computer criteria for overdrafts were altered, and the company was given a month to reduce its overdraft at the very moment when they had been going to apply for an increased one.

A loan from a High Street bank may be sensible, but financing through an overdraft from a High Street bank is becoming increasingly risky.

If you do wish to apply for a loan, first check that the interest rate to be charged is not more expensive than other sources of finance. If the interest rate seems reasonable then a High Street bank can often give a reasonably quick decision on a loan. This is especially the case if you are applying for a Loan Guarantee Scheme (LGS). You will need to make a formal loan proposal complete with a business plan and the latest set of management accounts. You may be able to prepare both through using a simple software package costing under £100 such as PlanIT Business Plan from Software Warehouse, Tel: 01675 468 330. This will enable you to produce a formal business plan in a day, assuming you have all the figures to hand.

If you already have a loan or overdraft from a High Street bank, you may be able to make considerable savings in interest if you are able to switch to an alternative source of finance. Check with some of the finance sources listed below.

Central schemes

You may be able to get grants in place of loans. Regional Enterprise Grants, grants in Development Areas, grants from the European Regional Development Fund and grants through the Rural Development Commission are all available if you qualify. Details can be obtained through the Department of Trade and Industry, 1 Victoria Street, London SW1H 0ET, who can provide a brochure on Regional Enterprise Grants and a leaflet *The Regional Initiative – Guide to Regional Selective Assistance.*

A grant may cut your borrowing costs to nil!

Financial companies

This is a broad heading consisting of accountancy companies that specialise in obtaining finance for small- to medium-sized companies. Many of them are also business advisers. You will find them under 'Accountants', in *Yellow Pages*. Examples are Arthur Andersen, BDO Stoy Hayward, Coopers & Lybrand, Deloitte and Touche, Ernst & Young, KPMG, Price Waterhouse, to name only a few. These companies may charge a little more than your local accountant for producing your accounts, but if you are likely to require finance in the future, they are an ideal choice as accountants. They will know your company and your financial situation and will be well placed to offer suitable finance when you require it. They will also know the local financial market and where potential investors may be found. Many of them operate world-wide and can give advice on finance for exporting.

Venture capital companies

Venture capitalists normally take a minority stake in a company and appoint a nominee to the board. This means that they have a continuing involvement with the running of the company. This can be a mixed blessing! The experience such directors can bring is invaluable, but you may not welcome outside advice! On the positive side the cost to you of venture capital is usually low. Venture capitalists make their money from the increasing value of their stake in the company rather than the interest on their investment. They will usually provide a considerable cost savings over finance from a bank.

A directory of venture capitalists is available from the British Venture Capital Association, Essex House, 12–13 Essex Street, London WC2R 3AA, Tel: 0171 240 3846.

Investment companies

For this chapter these will be defined as companies set up specifically for the purpose of investment in small- to medium-sized companies.

The main example is 3i who provide equity and long-term loan capital where the sum required is in excess of £100,000, and the company requiring finance has a turnover in excess of £1 million. Their head office is at 91 Waterloo Road, London SE1 8XP, Tel: 0171 928 3131.

3i have offices throughout the UK. They state that they are risk takers and share the entrepreneurial attitudes of the companies they back. My experience of several companies that they have helped is that the companies are encouraged to run themselves efficiently with a minimum of 'interference' from 3i. Usually a director is appointed to the board to safeguard 3i interests and offer advice. The company is usually offered several suitable directors to choose from, the compatibility of the director and the company being considered extremely important.

Shareholders

If you have investing shareholders, then they should always be first on your list for obtaining finance. Shareholders may well be willing to invest capital to provide you with extra finance. Such capital may be provided as a straight loan, or through preference or ordinary shares. You should take advice from your accountant and solicitor about the best method. In many cases the finance can be 'geared' to a shareholding. For example, investors may be offered 1000 extra shares at £3 each if they provide a low interest loan of £50,000.

'Angels'

Angels are individuals or groups of individuals who invest in small- to medium-sized companies in order to provide extra capital. Often they will provide a low interest loan coupled with a shareholding as detailed above under 'shareholders'. They will become shareholders. Angels also have considerable management skills to put into the business. Many are retired senior managers from large companies. Your accountant or bank may have contact with angels, or you can contact LINC (Local Investment Networking Company Ltd). Their head office is London Enterprise Agency, 4 Snow Hill, London EC1A 2BS, Tel: 0171 236 3000 and they have several regional offices.

LINC was established as a not-for-profit organisation sponsored by Midland, NatWest, Barclays, The Royal Bank of Scotland and Kingston Smith. It specialises in matching private investors with companies seeking equity funding of between £10,000 and £250,000. LINC operates a database for matching companies and investors, and also hosts meetings where companies can give a presentation to potential investors.

Financing through angels or shareholders is usually the lowest cost method of finance. You also have the advantage of potential advice from your new shareholders!

Remember – always try several sources of finance and compare costs. This is particularly important where you are considering your High Street bank. Investment through existing shareholders or angels will usually give cost savings over other sources, but you will normally have to give up a little of your control. You should discuss your requirement with your accountant. The above is only a small selection of finance sources and your accountant will know of others which may be more tailored to your precise situation.

OVERDRAFTS VERSUS LOANS

You should discuss these alternatives with your bank manager and your accountant. Overdrafts may often be cheaper than a loan, but they are less secure as they can be reduced at any time. Now that banks are tending to use computers rather than people to evaluate lending risk, reduction of overdraft facilities seems to be happening more often! Loans may cost more, but the conditions of a loan are usually fixed and you are less likely to find it disappearing or reducing.

It is always worth discussing your requirements with more than one bank. Bank policies change, and at any given time one bank may be offering much more favourable terms than another. Since your borrowing may represent a sizeable chunk of your profits, time spent on your decision is management time put to very effective use.

Advantages of a loan:

- Conditions are laid down at the start. You usually have the security of knowing that the loan cannot suddenly be withdrawn.
- Interest rates can usually be fixed if you need to ensure fixed costs of borrowing.

Advantages of an overdraft:

- Overdrafts are flexible. The ability to reduce them when you have spare cash means that borrowing costs are minimised.
- Overdrafts are usually cheaper in the long run.

LEASING AND RENTING RATHER THAN BUYING

The leasing, renting or buying of vehicles is dealt with in Chapter 4. The same decision applies to equipment used inside the organisation. It is often more cost effective to lease or rent equipment rather than spend capital. If you have spare capital or access to cheap loans it probably makes more sense to buy. This will cut the cost of leasing or renting. If you have no spare capital, and any loan would be expensive, it may make sense to lease or rent. It will cut the costs of expensive loans or overdrafts. Most equipment from photocopiers to large items of manufacturing equipment can be leased or rented.

Because the considerations are complex and usually involve looking at tax liability, you should discuss the options with your accountant. You need to look at the options, do not ignore them. The correct choice of buy, lease or rent can cut your costs considerably.

STOCK CONTROL

We dealt with stocks and just in time (JIT) ordering briefly in Chapter 2. The value of stocks in many organisations is high and represents a significant element of the usage of cash. Many organisations are, in effect, borrowing money to finance their stocks. Stock may also be costing money by using storage space, heating, lighting and staff. Cost can be cut by reducing stocks.

It may not be sensible to reduce stocks in many cases. If you are selling 12-month-old mature Cheddar cheese there will be no point in reducing your stocks if that means that the Cheddar will only be four months old and mild! If you have to give customers a quick and speedy service, you may hold sizeable stocks to ensure that you can supply 95% of requirements within 24 hours. Cutting stocks might reduce your service to unacceptable levels.

If you are to cut stock cost sensibly, then it will be necessary to find out the minimum level of stock that allows you to operate to acceptable standards. You will also need to find out the critical 20% of items that make up 80% of your stock value (this is called the Pareto principle). If you can focus on this 20% of items it will make your task easier.

The Toyota Motor Company in Japan started JIT stock systems many years ago. This system has now been followed world-wide. The system can lead to considerable cost savings and quality improvements but takes considerable time and commitment. It is not a 'quick fix'. A full JIT system will require expert help to install. The basics of JIT are:

- The change of relationships with suppliers from the usual Western 'combative' style of aggressive negotiations to one of mutual co-operation and trust. Supplier and customer work together to achieve the best results.
- The improvement of the quality of supplies so that no buffer stock is required to cover rejects.
- Precise planning and scheduling so that requirements from suppliers are forecast accurately.
- The ordering of stock to arrive only when actually required for the process so that no buffer stocks are held.

All this implies a culture change in the organisation that can only be achieved over an extended period of time. In the long term it will be very beneficial.

For short-term reduction in stock levels in order to cut costs you will need to make a detailed examination of your stocks. If you do not have accurate up-to-date stock records, this will not be possible. Complete stock records are essential. If you do not already have them, then this must be your first task. Once records have been produced get stock under control by:

- Identifying the 20% of lines that account for 80% of stock. Check each one individually to establish a sensible level.
- Examining your production or usage patterns to determine whether there are times when you need more or less of each item. There is no use holding stocks for a summer peak during the winter! Consult your customers or internal users to ensure that your stock usage is accurate.
- Separating customers/internal users into those who have to have a speedy delivery (they may be operating a JIT system) and those who can accept a delay. A delay will mean that you will be able to run out of stock of supplies occasionally and wait until new stocks arrive. This will mean that you can carry reduced stocks. Some customers may accept a delayed delivery time in return for a small discount.
- Never ordering automatically once a month – order when you need to.
- Shortening purchase lead times through discussions with your suppliers. Try to find ways of ensuring your supplier carries stocks, not you.
- Monitoring stocks continually and ordering when a predetermined trigger point is reached. This will require a formal stock reordering system. This does not need to be complicated. A simple card placed with stock to be handed to the order department when a certain level is reached is all that is needed.

DEBTOR CONTROL

Credit control is crucial to cash flow. It is also costly if not controlled tightly. Many organisations can cut costs simply by controlling debtors more carefully. Money that is owing to you is money that could be used to earn interest, repay overdrafts and reduce interest payments, earn early payment discounts from suppliers, invest in cost saving equipment. You need that money!

In all but the very smallest organisations, debtor control means having a suitable accounting system (see Chapter 5 on Information Technology (IT)). Such systems for a small organisation need only cost £100 or so and will pay for themselves many times over. The accounting system will produce an 'aged debtors' list' showing who owes what, and how much is overdue. Many packages will automatically produce a chasing letter. Always chase up overdue money. One company that I know sends a chasing letter immediately money is overdue and follows with a solicitors' letter if the money is not paid within 14 days. They have an arrangement with a firm of local solicitors who have a computer system that produces a standard solicitors' letter for under £8. Further expense is only incurred if legal action is actually required. Most companies pay immediately on receipt of the solicitors' letter.

Work out a schedule for chasing and stick to it. An ideal format is:

Item	Action and timing	Note
Invoice	Immediately goods are despatched/service provided	
Statement	Regularly on a fixed day each month	
Aged debtors' list	Run off once a week	Examine each week. Decide on action on overdue amounts
Letter	Send 7 to 14 days after payment is due	This should just be a polite reminder
Phone call	7 days after the letter	Discuss why the payment has not been made. Get a firm agreement for immediate payment
Final letter	7 days after the date agreed in the telephone call	A very firm letter stating that matters will be placed in the hands of your solicitor if payment is not received within 48 hours. Stop any further supplies
Solicitors' letter	3 days after final letter	

You will wish to alter the above to fit your own needs. Once you have established a procedure, *stick to it*, with no exceptions. Your customers have no grounds for complaint if they have agreed to payment terms when they placed the order.

If all else fails, remember that you can use the small claims court, which can achieve remarkable results at minimal costs.

You may wish to avoid all the problems of debtors by factoring your invoices. This means that your sales ledger is passed to an outside firm who will pay you all money owing to you on time and assume the responsibility of getting the money from your customers. This has many advantages but costs money. The cost will depend on the record for payment of your customers but is unlikely to cost less than 1% of invoice totals. Your bank may be able to provide such a service – or you can use specialist firms such as Alex Lawrie – look under 'Factoring and invoice discounting' in *Yellow Pages*.

CREDITOR CONTROL

If you can extend the time that you take to pay your bills, you will have the same effect as getting your cash from debtors quickly. You will cut costs of overdrafts and loans. This section is headed creditor *control* and not creditor cheating! This means that where you take longer to pay, it should be by agreement. If you are continually late in paying bills you will earn a poor reputation with suppliers who will consider you a bad risk and may even increase the prices that they charge you to cover the length of payment.

You can achieve the maximum credit by concentrating on the 20% of your suppliers that account for 80% of your credit by:

- Timing deliveries for the end of the month. Usually this will mean that they will be invoiced the next month. Many companies have terms of payment at the end of the month following the invoice. Find out the terms of each major supplier and time your orders accordingly.
- Discussing payment terms with major suppliers. You may be able to extend terms from 28 days to the end of the month following, from 30 days to 60 days. If a supplier knows that you are a good payer, and will always pay inside the agreed time, then you may be able to negotiate extended terms.
- Ask for a discount for prompt payment. Many companies which have 28-day terms may allow a discount of 1.5–2.5% for settlement in 7 or 14 days. If you can borrow money for less then this (and you almost

certainly can) or have cash available, then this will cut the cost of your purchase.

- Making special arrangements favourable to your supplier in return for longer credit. For example, you may agree to a slight change in specification, delivery size or timing which helps your supplier, in return for extended credit. So long as the changes do not affect you adversely, you will have cut costs through extending your credit with the supplier.

Many organisations are unwilling to discuss trading terms with their suppliers. They feel that they are unlikely to achieve anything. The reverse is true. If you target the critical 20% of suppliers you will be surprised at the cost savings that can be made just by having a firm discussion.

BUDGETS AND CASH FLOW AS A COST CUTTING TOOL

Budgets and cash flow go together. In order to produce an accurate cash flow forecast you must first produce a budget.

An accurate cash flow forecast will enable you to schedule your operations in such a way as to maximise the cash in your business and minimise the requirement for overdrafts and loans. This will cut your cost of borrowing. Most important of all, it will indicate times when you may be in danger of exceeding your borrowing ability and in risk of becoming insolvent.

If you are not producing a regular monthly cash flow forecast, then you are living dangerously! If you are in a cash business such as a shop, then you need weekly forecasts.

The first step is to produce a budget. Budgets are normally produced on an annual basis but most cash flows are for a running 12-month period. This means that as you go through a budget year you should be forecasting your budget for 12 months ahead in order to produce your cash flow. It is dangerous merely to repeat your income and expenditure month by month, rather than actually calculating an accurate budget figure.

I am not going to outline the methods of producing a budget and cash flow in this book. This is a specialist subject and one that should be discussed with your accountant. Suitable books are *Financial Management for the Small Business* by Colin Barrow and *Finance for the Non-financial Manager* by John Harrison. There are many other suitable books which will be available from your local bookshop and library.

SUMMARY

Finance and stocks are the areas that usually 'make or break' an organisation. If you have accurate records of cash flow and stocks, and revue them regularly (at least monthly), then you will have the information which will enable you to survive. Regular analysis of cash flow and stocks will indicate the areas where cost savings can be effected.

Savings can usually be effected in the way in which you handle your bank account. Analysis of the way in which you handle deposits, payments and loans, will normally lead to cost savings.

Consider carefully the options of purchase, hire and lease. There are often significant differences in costs and the correct choice can save you money.

If you require finance, there are many alternatives from which to choose. The right choice can cut your finance costs considerably. You may be able to cut the requirement for finance from your savings in stocks and cash flow.

Careful analysis and control of debtors and creditors can lead to substantial savings in the cost of your overdraft.

Always consult your accountant before making decisions; there are often hidden implications in a course of action, particularly in the area of taxation.

FOUR

ADMINISTRATION

I am using 'administration' to cover a wide range of areas not specifically covered in other chapters. These include office activities, premises, utility costs, services, general outgoings, company vehicles, etc. Although each area may only amount to a small expenditure, there are considerable savings to be made when these areas are added up. Often savings under these headings tend to be ignored as they are not the responsibility of any one senior person and there may not be specific budgets.

PREMISES

Selling

Many organisations ignore the value of their premises. Money tied up in property may well be better used in other areas of activity. Increasingly organisations are considering the possibility of selling their premises and renting back. The purchasing organisation may also be willing to take over repairs and maintenance. This is a complex operation and you should obtain advice from your accountant or other financial adviser. In particular you may find that loans or overdrafts are secured on the premises. The process has the following advantages:

- Your capital in the premises will be released. This may enable you to pay off an overdraft or loan (in fact you may have to do this if the premises were security). This can save more in interest than you have to pay for the lease.
- With released capital you may be able to invest in new equipment and stock which will enable you to make cost savings.
- You will be able to concentrate on your main business and not have to spend time on property matters such as maintenance. The new prop-

erty owner may well be able, through efficiency, to charge you less for maintenance than you were previously paying.
- You may be able to negotiate a short lease enabling you to move to different sized premises when this suits.

See 'Useful Addresses' section at the back of the book for further information: both ABB Building Service Ltd and Tarmac Servicemaster Ltd provide such a service.

You could also consider taking out a commercial mortgage on your property. This could release capital which you could invest to achieve cost savings. It might also be used to pay off an expensive overdraft. A suitable starting point would be your bank. Alternatively try Mortgages for Business: see 'Useful Addresses' at the back of this book.

Maintenance

It is often possible to arrange for all maintenance of your premises to be undertaken by a specialist company. This often cuts costs as the specialist company buys in bulk and has flexible staff, whereas you may have to use maintenance staff who are not always fully employed. It is sometimes possible to contract on a basis where you are guaranteed savings. It is well worth getting a quotation from a suitable company. You will find one in *Yellow Pages*.

Letting out

If you have spare space in your premises, you may be able to generate an income by letting this out to someone else. If you have spare capacity in your clerical staff, you may be prepared to offer a 'serviced' space which provides telephone answering and secretarial services. This usually commands a high rental and is in great demand. It does not matter how small the space is. I am writing this in a small room rented in an industrial complex. I am happy to pay for a room where I can retreat and write undisturbed! The rental includes all services and there are at least 20 other people on the complex renting spare offices, workshops or storage space. The owners of the complex have generated a considerable income by renting out unwanted space. All the rentals are for six months, then one month's notice. This enables the company to get back premises that it needs for its own purposes at short notice.

If you are considering letting out premises you should only do so by means of a formal agreement drawn up by your solicitor. You do not want to find that you are unable to get rid of an unwelcome tenant! Ensure the maximum income by:

- Offering small units at a high rental. Three offices will fetch a higher rental if rented to three individuals than if rented out as a suite of three offices.
- Offering services to accompany the rental. Telephone answering, secretarial services, mail forwarding, meeting room facilities and provision of coffee and tea, are all profitable services to offer. You may wish to make the extra charge for services a 'compulsory' extra.
- Only offering short-term rentals. This enables you to rent to someone else if your existing tenant proves unsuitable. It also enables you to raise rentals regularly if demand increases.
- Offering furnished premises if you have spare equipment/furniture. Most people wanting such accommodation will pay a considerable extra rental to avoid having to buy furniture themselves. Turn your unwanted desks into rental income!
- Using a standard lease so that you only have the expense of legal advice once when you create the first lease.
- You may be able to dispense with legal advice if you use a reputable commercial property agency to find customers for you. They will probably have a standard lease on file. They may also be able to get you a higher rental which will more than cover their charges.

You may be able to rent out to someone who can provide you with a valuable service. A company that I know had a small printing department that was used to print labels, boxes and instruction leaflets. They rented out the unit and sold the equipment to someone wishing to set up as a printer. They received rental for the premises, sold the printing machine to the printer and saved staff costs on printing. Their printing costs were halved and they received a high rental for the premises.

Renting

You may wish to rent temporary premises to cut costs in your own organisation. In particular you may wish to rent short term to accommodate production for a special order, storage space to take advantage of a special purchase opportunity, or temporary space for extra staff taken on for a particular contract. Renting short term may save money compared to moving to larger premises, forgoing a contract, passing up a special purchase opportunity or having to contract out to someone else because you do not have the room that you temporarily need.

SERVICES

Selling

You may well be able to cut costs by selling administration services to other organisations. This will cut your staff and overhead costs. The potential for this will depend on your circumstances, but areas for investigation should include:

Use of complex office equipment

If you have a photocopier that will copy and collate 20 copies of a 50-page document then you may be able to sell this service to other local organisations. Colour photocopiers, A2 copiers, binders, stitchers and laminators are also possible sources of revenue. Selling time on these machines will cut your own usage costs.

You could prepare a small brochure offering your equipment (and operating staff) for rent by the hour or per task.

Use of spare administration staff

If you have administration staff not fully occupied, it may be possible to sell their services. With modern telecommunication systems, for example, your switchboard may be able to take on tasks for other organisations. Small local organisations may welcome the ability to divert their calls to your switchboard when they are out. Individuals working on their own would welcome call diversion and secretarial services, possibly even bookkeeping.

If you have staff only 75% utilised, then consider cutting your staffing costs by selling the spare 25%. You will be able to charge above the normal staff rate for such services. You may well be able to sell the spare 25% of your labour costs for 40%, cutting your costs even further.

You will need to ensure that selling the services of staff and equipment does not take precedence over the demands of your own business and that you still have the spare capacity to deal with your own peak demand.

Buying in

If you have a variable workload you have the choice of employing extra staff to cope with peaks, or buying in the service of staff only at peak times. It may well cut costs if you employ the minimum of staff and buy in at peak times. In the same way it may cut costs to buy in staff for holiday cover rather than 'make do' with a lower level of staffing over holidays. Possible approaches are:

- Use a temporary staff agency to provide cover when required. This is the most expensive option.
- Find a pool of people locally willing to work part time when required. It is surprising how many people are willing to do this.
- Use staff from a local organisation who are temporarily overstaffed.
- Consider employing someone jointly with another local organisation with costs allocated between you according to usage.

OUTGOINGS

Post

You can cut down on staff usage by:

- Using a franking machine rather than stamps if you have a very large outgoing post. Remember that the franking machine costs money; you have to have it 'recharged' when your credit runs out and you will have to re-ink etc at regular intervals. It is only worth while for high volumes. Many Post Offices will frank letters free of charge which saves labour sticking on stamps.
- If you have a large mailing list, check for duplications. It is surprising how often people receive several identical mailings from the same company. In addition you should on some regular basis (depending on the frequency of your mailings) check that addressees actually want your mailings. You could, for example, enclose a letter with your next mailing stating that no more mailings will be sent unless requested by returning a reply-paid card. Although this is an initial high cost, you will cut costs in the long run if you do regular mailings. If you do mailings at least quarterly you will almost certainly save costs by an annual check in this way.
- Consider using mail rather than couriers or delivery services. The Post Office offers various fast guaranteed services for home and overseas deliveries. They are always cheaper than courier or delivery services.
- Ensure that first-class post is only used when absolutely necessary. Does it really matter if a letter takes two days rather than one?
- Ensure that you use the cheapest post classification. It may be cheaper to send by first or second class rather than parcel post (depending on weight).

- Could you use a card rather than a letter? A card saves on envelope and envelope stuffing costs.
- Would it be cheaper to send a fax? Fax is usually cheaper (and much quicker) if only one or two pages are involved.
- If you are sending a heavy parcel by post, check that it is not cheaper to send by TNT or a similar delivery service – it often is.

Telephone

Your biggest cost saving might be made by transferring to a different telephone company. Most organisations now have a choice between British Telecommunications, Mercury and a regional cable company. Some areas may have a local microwave service or other provider. You should ask for alternative suppliers to give a cost estimate based on your last telephone bill. Savings of 10–20% can often be made by transferring to a different provider. Check that you can take your existing number with you. If not you will have to deduct the cost of reprinting/amending stationery and notifying customers and suppliers from any potential cost savings.

Some other areas of cost saving are:

- If you regularly send a large number of faxes then consider a fax machine that will allow you to store faxes and send them automatically at a cheap rate. If you send or receive a large number of faxes and use a roll paper machine, then you will also save money by switching to a plain paper machine.
- In order to stop staff being diverted from tasks by phone calls (which costs money!) install a voice mail system with an individual voice box for each member of staff. These are now available at very low cost and enable staff to pick up messages at a time when they are not doing urgent work.
- If you have several members of staff then consider an automatic switchboard where callers can forward calls to individual members of staff (or departments) through using a tone phone. This can cut costs by eliminating the need for a switchboard operator. One member of staff will need to be nominated as a general enquiry point for those callers who do not want to be forwarded to an individual or who do not have a tone phone.
- Some modern systems enable you to list all calls made from each extension phone. This means that you can check on private phone calls and provide each member of staff with a printout of calls and a target of reducing their total bill by a percentage. Once staff are regularly issued with such printouts, costs usually reduce considerably! If

you do not have such a system, ask for an itemised telephone bill. Examining this bill will enable you to identify regularly called numbers and check that they are business calls. Check unusually long calls to see if there is any way that they can be made shorter and ensure that there are no chat-line numbers being called.

- Hold a training session for all staff to explain the considerable savings that can be made by keeping calls short. Suggest that staff do not hold if someone is engaged, but call back later. Also suggest that they try and find staff for whom there are calls rather than saying 'x will call you back' – at your expense! Ask staff for suggestions on how to cut down on the time of calls; this will lead to a discussion on alternative methods that will ensure everyone is call-time conscious!
- If you have an answerphone do not leave a general announcement that asks callers to leave a message after the tone. Try and be specific: 'We are closed for lunch until 2 pm, please call back after 2 pm or if the matter is very urgent leave a message after the tone.' This ensures a minimum of messages for you to answer on your phone bill, ensures the maximum of people call back at their expense, yet at the same time allows those who wish to leave a message.

Subscriptions

Many organisations have subscriptions to organisations that they never use and periodicals that they never read. In addition there are some 'trade' directories that send invoices for entries that are paid automatically without checking that the entry is required.

- Issue instructions that no magazine or journal subscriptions, or directory entries, are to be paid without authorisation.
- Draw up a list of all magazine and journal subscriptions. Check that they are all really necessary. Eliminate duplicates and set up a circulation list for those read by several people. Newspapers also cost money – ensure that only essential ones are ordered.
- Check any subscriptions to organisations and societies. Are they really necessary?

Services

Many organisations have contracted services for cleaning, coffee, plants etc. Check whether these services are really needed, and whether the frequency is suitable.

For example, many cleaning services are for a daily clean where a weekly clean would be quite satisfactory. Coffee making may be contracted out where a member of staff has time spare to make coffee. Even when your own staff carry out cleaning it may be possible to save money by rearranging the frequency of cleaning. Break down the building(s) into separate areas and determine the correct cleaning frequency for each area. Often the only real task carried out when cleaning daily is the emptying of each waste-paper basket! Put a large bag bin in each area and instruct staff to empty their waste-paper baskets into it when leaving. This way you may be able to reduce cleaning to weekly in all areas, at a considerable cost saving.

You will find details of cleaning companies in *Yellow Pages*. Try Cooper Cleaning Ltd: see 'Useful Addresses' at the back of this book.

COMPANY VEHICLES AND TRAVEL

Cars

The situation with company cars is complex and if you have several vehicles it is well worth consulting the fleet experts from a major car manufacturer or large dealership. The options open include:

- Outright purchase of a vehicle.
- Leasing.
- Obtaining a loan to purchase.
- Giving a car allowance, or increase in salary, to the employee who then buys a vehicle.
- Renting.

It is not possible to give precise advice because the tax situation is constantly changing, and the situation from tax and operating points of view are different for each company. The position also alters from the employees' point of view. If a straight salary increase is given then it will be pensionable; if a car allowance, or salary in lieu is given then the tax and pension positions are more complex.

Considerable money can be saved by taking expert advice.

Company vehicles

Company vehicles (other than cars) are usually vans, lorries and artics. Here the choices are:

- Buy outright.

- Rent.
- Lease.
- Use contractor.
- Employ owner-driver.

The choices between buying and leasing are again the area where expert advice is best as the situation is continually altering. Your accountant can also help here with advice on which is most tax effective in your situation.

Renting can be useful where a vehicle is regularly required for short periods, where delivery is seasonal or where use is only occasional. Sometimes a particular contract will have delivery requirements that will temporarily require extra vehicles. Although renting in these circumstances may seem expensive, it is usually much cheaper than the purchase of a vehicle which will not be fully utilised. In addition rental is fully allowable as a business expense for tax purposes.

A contractor is often even more cost effective than a rented vehicle. The payment will only be made for each specific delivery and a driver will be provided by the contractor. It is often possible to combine loads with other organisations on the vehicle and it is also often possible to utilise a 'back load' when a contractor is delivering in your area. It is worth while consulting a transport agent or consultant from *Yellow Pages* – they can sometimes arrange very advantageous prices. The more flexible you can be with pick up and delivery times, the more likely you are to get a low price.

Owner-drivers are sometimes the most cost-effective method. The normal system is that the owner-driver is contracted to work for you. He or she may even be required to have his or her vehicle painted in your livery. The advantages to you are:

- You will have a transport charge made which is an allowable expense.
- You will not be responsible for the capital outlay on the vehicle.
- You will not be responsible for staff costs (National Insurance etc) for the driver.
- From the customer's point of view it appears to be your vehicle and driver.
- The situation is flexible. If you do not fully utilise the vehicle the owner may be able to do other contract work to keep his or her charges low.

It must be emphasised that it is not possible to give specific advice because of tax regulation changes. You are advised to seek the advice of a transport expert and your accountant. In almost every case a close examination of transport policy will provide considerable savings.

Travel

Cost savings can be made in travel by:

- Comparing methods and choosing the best. In many cases there is a choice between car, air and rail. In some cases a coach should also be considered. It may be that rail will beat a car for time and cost. Often air beats rail on cost if a cheap air fare is chosen. All too often a car is chosen for convenience but takes longer, is more expensive and far more stressful than other forms of transport.
- Shopping around for the best price. At the time of writing the return air fare from London to Glasgow varies from approximately £220 to £49 depending on the deal. If you are prepared to tie yourself down to specific flights then you can usually make a large cost saving. There are similar savings to be made on rail and coach travel.
- Buying travel vouchers. If you are a large user of transport you can buy vouchers for travel at a discount from rail, air and coach operators.
- Obtaining a discount from an agent for regular use. You do not always have to be a large user. Your local travel agent (see *Yellow Pages*) will also be able to access details of cheap fares easily and advise on the best method of travel.

Hotels

Savings can often be made on hotel bills by the following:

- Asking for a lower price or discount when booking. Recently a friend made a late booking for a hotel at 6 pm on the night. He was told the price was £75. He replied that he was not prepared to pay that, and as the room was obviously empty the hotel might consider a lower price. He got the room for £59. There is no harm in asking!
- Investing in a hotel guide – often a local independent hotel will be listed that charges much lower prices than a large chain. The service will usually be more personal as well.
- Phoning a business contact in the area and asking for a recommendation.
- Booking through a travel agent who may have negotiated discounts with hotel groups.
- If you are a large user of hotels most main groups will offer a discount.
- When travelling abroad there are many package deals available through a travel agent offering travel plus accommodation – even for a single overnight stay.

ENERGY COSTS

It is usually possible to make significant savings in energy costs. There are many energy consultants who will make a survey and advise on cost savings. They usually have access to sophisticated analysis systems and will often make no charge unless they can more than cover their costs by the savings. You will find them in *Yellow Pages*. It is cost effective to try and make the most obvious savings yourself first.

Gas

There are now several gas companies competing for business; many have considerably lower prices than British Gas. Some will supply all users, others will only supply users with a consumption greater than around £1500 pa. It is certainly worth while investigating alternative suppliers of gas. At the same time, make sure that you contact British Gas and get details of alternative tariffs that may save costs.

If you are using gas for heating then you can save considerable amounts of money by using suitable controls. These can include:

- Zone controls. Some areas of your business may not be in continuous use. Offices, for example, may only be open from Monday to Friday whilst the production area operates seven days a week. Valves that segment the building into zones can be switched to timers to ensure that only areas in use are heated.
- Time/date switches. These ensure that the heating system is switched off when the heat is not required. Check the settings. Often the timer is set to switch off late at night when no one has been in the building for hours.
- Thermostats. There should be at least one thermostat controlling each heating zone. An adjustment downwards of only 1°C can result in considerable savings. Individual controls in each room or on each radiator will usually recoup their cost and start making savings within a year or so.
- Hot water storage tanks – see below under 'Electricity'.

In addition you should appoint one member of staff as 'energy saver'. They should be responsible for checking that timers, thermostats and zone controls are set correctly. They may need training to do this.

Electricity

At present there are no viable alternatives for small businesses for normal electricity supply, although if you are a very large user you may be able to negotiate with rival supply companies. Cost saving methods include:

- The use of thermostats and timers (as above) for gas.
- Auto cut-off controls. For corridors and staircases that are rarely used an auto cut-off to switch off lights after, say three minutes, will save money without endangering safety. In production areas you may have machinery that uses current when not being operated (heat sealers, coolers etc). A cut-off switch will ensure that energy is not being wasted when the machine has not been operated for some time.
- If you have old machinery that consumes large amounts of electricity you may be able to make savings by upgrading to a low-usage model. You may be able to pay for the machine in quite a short time from energy savings and you may well get an improved model into the bargain.
- Start a staff education campaign. Appoint a member of staff to run it. The simplest ideas work best. Put notices on equipment stating electricity usage – 'I use 14p an hour', and 'Please turn me off after use' for lights etc. Once electricity savings become clear, post notices telling staff that the campaign has worked. If savings are large you might consider putting some money towards the annual Christmas party (or something similar) to enable staff to benefit from their efforts.
- If you have hot water storage tanks, either insulate them very well or change to a hot water on demand system (such as individual water heaters for wash basins); storing hot water is expensive.

Some organisations generate electricity from wind and water power, or from an on-site generating plant. If you are generating electricity for any purpose then you can make arrangements to sell your surplus back to your electricity company. This is particularly valuable if you are generating from wind or water power.

Oil

Depending on circumstances, oil may be a cheap form of energy or not. It is worth while getting quotations for converting from oil to gas or electricity. If you decide to, or have to, stay with oil then you should regularly get quotations from several suppliers.

The same comments on controls apply as for gas above.

Water

You should first investigate alternative supplies of water. Your water company may not be the only source of supply. British Waterways derives a substantial part of its income from selling water from its canals and reservoirs to industry. The Rivers Authority also sells water. If you are a substantial user of water you should investigate the possibility of sinking your own bore holes. Check *Yellow Pages* for local well-borers and sinkers.

You will probably be paying for the water that you use through a meter. Worthwhile savings can be effected through:

- Checking flows to each section of your premises when all appliances are turned off. This checks for leaks and unknown usage. This should be done by a plumber with suitable equipment.
- Altering toilet cisterns to economy flush or replacing with economy cisterns.
- Fitting timers to urinal auto flush systems.
- Checking flow through major water usage equipment such as coolers and washers to see if the flow can safely be cut down.
- Recycling water through your equipment where this is possible. In some manufacturing processes it may be possible to run waste water through filters to suitable storage tank for reuse.
- Ensuring excess water is not being used by vehicle washing, garden maintenance.
- It is possible to get pressure-sensitive valves that will shut off the water supply to a section of your premises if a pipe bursts, a water pipe becomes disconnected from equipment or water is left full on for a predetermined period. An expert plumbing company can advise.

SUMMARY

The areas covered in this chapter are often neglected when trying to achieve cost savings. The reason seems to be twofold; the areas for making savings are not obvious and analysis is required before areas for savings can be identified. As the potential cost savings are large, the effort is well worth while. In addition, the analysis of your administration will point to areas where the performance of your organisation can be improved, leading to higher efficiency.

Do not assume that you should own your own premises, or even have sole occupancy of them. They are a valuable asset that can be used to cut your costs.

The choice of buy, rent or lease for vehicles is a complex one, but the right choice can offer considerable cost savings.

Travel costs need close control. Significant savings in fares and hotel costs can be made quite easily.

Utility costs are often overlooked but large savings, particularly in heating costs, can result from relatively small expenditure on suitable equipment.

FIVE

INFORMATION TECHNOLOGY (IT)

Many companies do not use information technology (IT) to cut costs yet it is one of the most effective methods of cost cutting. When IT is combined with a rationalisation of paperwork the cost cutting potential is increased. In order to consider the best methods of cost cutting, it is necessary to conduct a survey of paperwork and computer systems, and secretarial and clerical staff.

PAPERWORK

Paperwork system	Function
Invoicing system and chasing letters	Ensuring debtors' money is received on time

EQUIPMENT/SYSTEMS

Item	Function
PC- 386 desktop	Use as word processor by Eileen Fowler

STAFFING

Member of staff	Duties
Eileen Fowler	Secretary, types letters for Bob Smith and Jean Wescott, answers phone from 1–2 pm, responsible for petty cash

Although it will take time, this survey is essential. It will enable you to cut costs through trimming paperwork systems and staff to an optimum level. This may require investment in IT systems, but the cost of the IT investment is far outweighed by the cost savings.

PAPERWORK

It is necessary to start with paperwork as the level of paperwork largely determines the levels of staffing and IT requirements. In Chapter 8 we look at sales administration paperwork. In many companies there are separate paperwork systems for orders, production, delivery and accounts. These can often be combined into one system using one set of paperwork. In a fully computerised system the accounts package is often capable of doing this. If you are not computerised then a multi-part document can be created which is filled in at the time an order is received and follows through product and despatch (or service provision) to the final invoice, statement and reminder. Such multi-part documents are available from specialist business stationery suppliers or can be created by most commercial printers using carbonless paper. You can find your nearest printing company or specialist business stationery supplier in *Yellow Pages*.

Through using a linked system in this way, paperwork can be reduced and often staffing levels can also be reduced.

EQUIPMENT AND SOFTWARE

Paperwork can also be reduced through computerising some or all of the systems. There is no advantage in computerising a simple paperwork system which is already working well and using a minimum of staff. Computerisation is likely to require the purchase of suitable software and training of staff, which can be very expensive. More complex paperwork systems can show considerable cost savings when computerised, particularly in the area of accounts, management reports and balance sheet production. If computerisation is contemplated, then a check must first be made on what hardware is already available. You will have this information from the survey that you have completed.

A suitable standard 'entry' level business computer would be a Pentium 133, but a 486 66 would be perfectly capable of running any of the standard commercial software. Many programs will run perfectly on a 386 66. Check the minimum specification for software that you wish to run – you may find that your existing computer can run it. There is no point in spending money on a more 'powerful' computer that you do not need. You are likely to be able to upgrade your existing computer to increase performance. Increasing the memory and possibly substituting a faster processor is a very cost-effective way of improving performance without replacing the computer.

Some organisations are now changing to portable computers with a 'docking station' in the office. The portable computer can be used anywhere for document production, running programs and accessing or creating e-mail. When back in the office the portable computer is placed in the 'docking station' and converts to a desktop. With such a system a member of staff can work from home, a hotel bedroom, a train or virtually anywhere in the world in much the same way as they would work in the office.

Software is available which makes it possible for every member of staff to create their own letters and memos. The software can be used even by someone who cannot type. The computer is just switched on and instructions given by speaking into a microphone in the computer. The member of staff then dictates the letter or memo and the computer will arrange for it to be printed, faxed or sent by e-mail. The cost is only the equivalent of a couple of weeks' wages. A system of this type called Kurzweil Voice is sold by Talking Technologies (34 Glazbury Road, London W14 9AS, Tel: 0171 602 4107) at a cost of around £299. It interfaces with Microsoft Word, WordPerfect etc. They also sell one called Voicepad Pro for £79 that works with Windows WordPad. They also sell a program called Talk Back that will read documents, e-mail etc to you for around £79. IBM also produce an excellent system – Voice Type Dictation at around £79.

e-mail

e-mail is a system for sending messages and documents from one computer to another. The other computer can be in the same office, or in almost any country in the world. Some systems exist to send graphics and even video with an audio commentary to any computer in the world suitably equipped to receive them. e-mail can be via a software system such as Microsoft Mail™ or Lotus Notes™, or can be through the Internet.

Many organisations now use e-mail exclusively for internal memos and documents, and for many external documents as well. External e-mail can be sent from any computer with a modem but internal e-mail can normally only be sent if your computers are on a net. A net need only consist of two computers, so there is no reason not to be networked. Some advantages of a networked system are:

- Documents can be sent from one computer to another instantly.
- Programs and data can be shared between computers.
- e-mail is possible.
- Printers and modems can be shared between several computers.

Providing a network is simple, but unless you have your own computer expert, you will need to employ a computer engineer (find your local one in *Yellow Pages*). Each computer needs to be fitted with a network card and the computers connected together with a cable. Alternatively, you can have a ready-made network of one main file server computer plus five workstation computers provided for under £5000 (try Opus Technology PLC: see 'Useful Addresses'). The costs are more than justified by the time and cost savings you will be able to make when networked.

A more complex system is also available that can network desktops and portables and also provide dictation facilities for all the networked computers (ie you dictate your letters to the computer which then types them out). Try Hi-Grade (see 'Useful Addresses').

You do not have to have one computer for each member of staff. Many software systems make it possible for you to have one computer shared between several members of staff. Each staff member can have a password which will enable them to access their 'world' in the computer. They can have a very personalised screen and customised programs, and no one else will have entry to them. This system is ideal where there are part-time members of staff and infrequent users. Each user of the computer will have their own 'mail box' where e-mail can be sent.

A development of e-mail is voice mail where voice messages can be left in the recipient's 'mail box' either from another computer, or from the phone. In addition most systems allow a member of staff to access their mail box for voice and documents whilst they are at home. Voice can be accessed through a phone, but document access needs a computer and modem at home. If the member of staff has a portable computer and modem, then voice and mail boxes can be accessed from anywhere in the world (even where there is no phone if you have a satellite phone!).

The use of this e-mail access outside the office means that a member of staff need never be out of touch with the office. It is possible to work from home and yet receive e-mail, download documents and send work back to the office – all via e-mail or the Internet. This has led to many companies only providing one temporary desk for staff who normally work from home and this cuts costs considerably. Sales and service staff can operate from home with only occasional office visits needed for face-to-face discussions.

The Internet

Once an area for computer freaks, the Internet has now become an essential tool for many organisations. The Internet connects millions of computers world-wide. Once you have accessed the Internet you can communicate with all these computers at no extra cost. Once you have subscribed to an Internet service provider you are able to access the Internet via their server for a charge of a few pounds a month. Some suppliers also make a small charge per hour for the time that you are connected to the Internet. Connection to the server is normally at local telephone call rates and once connected you can send and receive information from all over the world at no extra cost. This means that you could send documents, pictures, sound and videos to someone in Australia, to be received almost instantly, for the price of a local phone call. One of the largest Internet suppliers is CompuServe: see 'Useful Addresses'.

You can also have your own 'page' on the Internet to provide information for your customers, advertise and receive messages from customers and potential customers world-wide. Try a specialist company like Software Warehouse: see 'Useful Addresses'.

The Internet can be used to send messages, data and documents, to place an advertisement or information. It can also be used to find information. Using one of the freely available 'search engines' means that you can type in a word and instantly be given a list of hundreds of documents available on the subject world-wide. You can then call up and read any of these documents. There is even an Internet *Yellow Pages* online to help you track down information under various headings.

You can get more details on the Internet by buying a suitable book such as *The UK Internet Book* by Sue Schofield.

All this means that it is usually much cheaper to send a document via the Internet than by post or courier. It will also be much quicker. Of course the recipient has also got to be able to access the Internet, but more and more businesses are now connected.

Networking your computers and connecting to the Internet will enable you to cut costs on paper, typing, telephone, fax and postage charges! You will, however, have to ensure that your staff are trained to use these new systems if you are going to get the full cost saving benefits. Training can be achieved by:

- Suitable books from your software supplier. Many are titled *The idiot's guide to . . .* or *The simple way to . . . .*

- CD disks giving interactive tutorials from your software supplier. You will need a CD drive on one of your computers. This should not cost more than £100-200 to fit (depending on type). You will probably need a sound card and speakers. Your local computer engineer will fit them.
- Courses run through your local technical college or by specialist companies. Try contacting Learning Tree International: see 'Useful Addresses'.

In even a small office, installing a network, connecting to the Internet and training staff will only cost a few hundred pounds, but will create considerable cost savings in the long run. In any locality there are always several computer engineers, specialists or consultants who can advise you – look in *Yellow Pages*.

STAFFING

From the above details you can see that there are many tools available to you to run your organisation with a minimum of paperwork and staff. In many cases there is no need for secretarial staff as individuals can create their own letters and transfer messages via e-mail or the Internet. They can do this from any location that they like. This means that use of e-mail, the Internet and software programs that allow staff to create their own letters and memos, will almost certainly enable you to reduce your staff.

From the survey you have carried out you should be able to determine what extra equipment, including hardware and software, is required, and the extent to which you can cut down on secretarial and clerical staff. In addition, the investment in suitable equipment will mean that each member of staff is far more productive which will cut overall company costs.

The main decision that you will have to make, after choosing your equipment, is the way in which your organisation will operate when it comes to letters and accounting systems. The choices are:

- Using secretaries for all external letters. If you are networked then the member of staff requiring a letter to be typed could dictate the letter on to their computer to be sent to the secretary (assuming a suitable voice transfer system is installed). Alternatively a draft letter could be sent to the secretary by e-mail. The secretary can return the final letter by e-mail for approval.
- Each member of staff types their own letters which are e-mailed to a secretary for final checking, printing and despatch.

- Each member of staff types and prints their own letters.
- Standard letters are available as templates on each computer and members of staff simply fill in the details to produce a final letter.
- Members of staff dictate their letters to their computer where a suitable software program (see under 'Equipment' above) converts to a letter.

The way in which you choose to operate will determine the equipment and staffing levels.

In the sections above we have primarily been looking at systems for transferring written documents. There are other IT systems which can link in and also cut costs.

ACCOUNTING SYSTEMS

As mentioned above there are several accounting systems which link sales orders to delivery notes, invoices, and the production of full accounts and management reports. A good example is Pegasus (contact Pegasus Software Ltd: see 'Useful Addresses'). In addition there are several simple accounting systems costing around £100, which can fully computerise the bookkeeping and invoicing functions, saving a considerable amount of staff time (for example Sage which is available from most software suppliers).

In these systems the creation of an order on the computer will automatically:

- Create a sales/service order which can be automatically sent to the correct department, representative or service provider.
- Order any stock required and if required initiate the production process.
- Provide despatch or service provision documents.
- Produce an invoice and reminder if required.
- Produce a statement.
- Produce management accounts, cash flows, annual accounts, balance sheet and any other reports required.

A purchase order will create a purchase order document and raise a cheque on the required date. It can also produce a goods received note and keep count of stock levels.

As you can see, such a system is capable of producing a considerable cost saving in staff in addition to ensuring closer control of your organisation. Such systems will also produce your VAT return and can be used to calculate PAYE and wages. For a small- to medium-sized company, the investment of from £100 for a simple system to £10,000 for a more complex system, plus staff training, is very small compared with the savings. In addition you will only need an external accountant at the year end to audit your figures. You may, therefore, also save a considerable amount of money in accountants' fees.

As a general rule of thumb, if you are employing the equivalent of one full-time person to produce your invoices, wages, VAT return, balance sheet or cash flow – or are using an external accountant to do any of these – you will save money by fully computerising your system. If you are not spending this amount of staff time, then you probably do not have sufficient control information to run your organisation properly! You need such a system!

Specialist systems

There are many systems specific to a particular business or organisation on the market. For example, there are systems for medical practices, retailers, dairy farms, production units, tyre fitters, bakers, solicitors, to name but a few. These systems have all been designed to save money through computerisation. You can usually find out details through trade or specialist magazines, your trade or professional association or *Yellow Pages* under 'Computer software'.

There are also many software packages for specialised functions usually costing under £100. Some examples are:

- *PlanIT Business Plan 2*. This produces a full business plan for presentation to your bank or other financial institution.
- *PlanIT Health and Safety*. This produces your own health and safety program.
- *PlanIT Letters and PlanIT Legal Letters*. Hundreds of letters that you can customise.
- *QuickAddress* from Royal Mail gives you the addresses for all postcodes. Just enter the postcode and the address appears.
- *Marketing Planner*. Produces a full marketing plan for your organisation.
- *Business Evaluator*. Evaluates your past, present and future performance. Includes all financial ratios including liquidity and survival ratio analysis.
- *Turbocad* enables you to produce technical drawings.
- *TurboProject* enables you to plan projects in great detail.

- *Microsoft Publisher* enables you to desktop-publish brochures, catalogues, leaflets, including artwork and photographs.
- *Globalink Power Translator* translates to and from French, Italian, Spanish and German as you type.

All these systems will save you a considerable amount of money over the manual method of achieving the same results.

If you are a small organisation then there will usually be an 'off the peg' item of software that you can use without modification. If you are a medium- to large-sized organisation then you may require the software to be customised to fit into your existing systems. Customisation by a computer consultant can be costly, but usually will still result in considerable cost savings.

PHONES AND FAX

You can save money on staff costs by installing equipment that will enable you to handle phone calls with minimum use of staff.

Does your organisation have an answer phone? If not it should have! A simple answer phone costing under £50 can be used to:

- Answer the phone when you are closed. This can save lost business! Customers can place orders and make enquiries 24 hours a day.
- Answer the phone when you are busy. Continually interrupting work to answer the phone is costly. An answer phone will take messages and let you ring back when you are less busy.

Alternatively, BT will provide an answering service that will even take calls when you are engaged. The cost is only a few pounds a quarter. In both cases you can access your messages from anywhere in the world. More complex answering machines can phone you at any number you request (ie home, a client etc) and tell you that there is a message waiting for you!

More complex systems (often computer based) will direct callers to the person they require without the use of a receptionist. Callers can be asked to 'press 1 for Mr Smith, 2 for Miss Jones' etc and the call will be routed to the correct person. Such systems can also be used to answer queries with pre-recorded information - 'press 4 for details of our surgery opening times', 'press 5 for a list of suppliers of our products' are examples. These systems can be obtained through BT or Mercury, or can be purchased as a software package such as PC Voice Mail 2000 at under £1000 from your local software supplier and run via your computer. You can eliminate a receptionist and staff answering some queries with this system.

These systems can also supply 'fax on demand'. This is a system for giving customers and clients information via fax. They dial in and are asked to press numbers on their fax keypad for various types of information. The information is stored on a computer and faxed directly back to the customer. The information can include illustrations and diagrams. This system saves on staff and postage and gives immediate information without the need to post the material. A simple fax system, that also includes facilities for answer-phone messages to choice, is Super Voice Pro which costs under £100.

Mobile phones

Although mobile phones can be very useful, they can also be very expensive to use. If your organisation uses mobile phones, consider the following:

- Place each phone on the low use tariff to save monthly rental (usually about £10 a month per phone can be saved in this way).
- Use the phone for inward calls only - outgoing calls should only be in an emergency. More than a few outgoing calls will negate the cost savings on monthly rentals as the rates will be higher.
- Check each bill monthly to ensure that personal calls are recharged to the user.
- Consider having a shared mobile which is taken out only as required and can, therefore, cover several members of staff. This will also have the advantage of removing personal tax liability from the users.

You should also consider removing all mobiles and replacing with pagers which can carry messages. These pagers can be bought outright from BT or Mercury and are available in many High Street stores. There is no monthly charge for use. Because messages can be sent and are readable on the pager display, there is usually no need to talk direct to the user who can use a public phone to call back when required.

Of course there are some staff that you may wish to continue carrying mobiles for security reasons.

The fax-modem option

Earlier in this chapter we looked at the advantages of e-mail, and mentioned that one of these is the ability to work anywhere in the world and still be able to keep in contact with the office. I am writing this chapter on a portable computer 350 miles from my house and office. I am able to contact my office by phone with my modem, plug into the network there and receive and send messages and faxes. Others are doing the same so that last night I received a message from Ethiopia and replied to it. The cost was a three-minute local phone call to receive all my messages and reply.

A modem is a small box which enables your computer to communicate with another computer or network over the telephone (including some mobile telephones). It will also send and receive faxes via your computer. A suitable modem costs under £80 (US Robotics Sportster Vi 14,000 speed plus fax). A suitable portable computer with a black and white screen (Toshiba T2110 486 75Mhz processor, 350Mb disk) costs under £700. A small, portable battery-operated bubble jet printer will cost around £170 (Hewlett Packard 340). All prices are exclusive of VAT. For under £1000 you should be able to equip a member of staff (or several if equipment is shared) to work anywhere. For suppliers, look in *Yellow Pages* or buy a copy of *Computer Shopper* which has hundreds of pages of advertisements.

What can this 'under £1000' system do? It should come with Windows 95™ loaded and this will give you a simple word processor plus modem control. For another £70 you can buy Microsoft Works which will give you a word processor, basic desktop publishing, a database and a spread-sheet. This will enable you to:

- Send and receive faxes.
- Send and receive e-mail from either your own network (if you have a modem on the network) or the Internet.
- Send and receive complex documents, spreadsheets, diagrams etc.
- Contact your office computer (if it or the network has a modem) and transfer files between the two computers.
- Prepare and print out documents (£30 will turn the printer into a full colour printer).
- Write and print out letters.
- Prepare and print out overhead projection slides for a presentation.
- Calculate costs while with a client, then print out proposals on the spot.

There are many more features. The computer can be used back in the office and connected to the office network. The £1000 investment will enable you to cut costs by increasing the productivity of staff, eliminate a lot of secretarial work, and the cost of producing and posting documents to members of staff. The system will work in most countries in the world through the Internet. Windows 95™ comes complete with an Internet connection (make sure you get Windows 95™ not Windows 3.1™).

No matter how small your organisation, you can almost certainly justify this system. Even if you work on your own you should consider this as your main computer. The addition of a full-sized keyboard and colour monitor for under £200 will turn it into a desktop computer. Alternatively, you could consider a colour portable with modem and CD-ROM built in. This will give you a fully portable multimedia computer for use anywhere and will cost around £2500 (Toshiba 410CDT).

The ultimate system

The ultimate system would be one which also allows you to dictate letters to your computer. Such a system costs around £3000 for the portable computer loaded with specialist software (try Hi-Grade: see 'Useful Addresses'). This system can recognise 200,000 English words, so is likely to be able to process all your documents without you touching a key! A secretary and communications system rolled into one at a price of only a few months of a secretary's salary. As the equipment will last for several years this must be a bargain cost saver.

Hi-Grade can also provide you with a network system of desktop and portable computers, all of which can use the dictation system, customised to your requirements complete with accounting packages.

WARNING Computer prices change very quickly with the fluctuating price of memory and processors. At the moment the trend is downwards by over 10% a year. The prices in this chapter are estimated 1997 prices and may well have changed by the time you read this book.

SUMMARY

Many people are afraid of technology, particularly computers, yet technology is probably the tool that offers you the way to make the greatest cost savings in your organisation.

Analysis of your requirements and help from an expert will enable you to choose a system of hardware and software that will significantly reduce costs by enabling your staff to operate more efficiently.

Communications are vital to any organisation, but unless controlled can be costly. An analysis of your communication methods and phone equipment can lead to significant cost savings.

Do not be frightened by information technology. You may not understand computers and feel that you will be unable to cope with the requirements of a computer system. It is much easier to operate a computer now compared with a couple of years ago. Windows 95, coupled with high-speed Pentium processors, have revolutionised the usability of computers. Many systems just require you to switch on and follow simple instructions.

If you are worried about computerising aspects of your organisation, you should contact a computer consultant or specialist from a large computer retailer for advice. Ask for a demonstration of the system before you buy it, and ask to see the accounting and other programs demonstrated before you make a choice. You will be surprised at the ease with which you can operate a modern system.

SIX

SALES AND DISTRIBUTION

In this chapter we will be looking at the price you can obtain for your product or service as an alternative to cost cutting. We will also be looking at ways of cutting costs in selling, sales forces, agents and distribution together with advertising.

PRICES

Although increasing price is not a method of cost cutting, increasing the price of a product or service reduces the need to cut costs. It is, therefore, an option that needs to be considered.

The first question to consider is whether altering the price for your product or service will alter the demand for it. If you are selling petrol then an increase in price will reduce sales and a reduction in price will increase sales. There will not be much point in increasing your price unless the extra profit will more than cover the loss in profit from lost sales. If you are the only hairdresser in town then you may be able to increase prices a little without losing any custom. People will have to go out of the town to find an alternative and this costs money.

What kind of business are you in? Can you increase prices a little without losing business? Often the only way to find out is by trying. There are some signs that would warn you not to:

- You are one of several similar businesses in the area and you have not got the majority of the business.
- You are the only business in the area, but your price is already higher than competitors nearby.
- You are in a business where it is known that price is very important.
- Your customers are already complaining about your high prices.
- Even a small drop in demand will have a bad effect on your business.

- You have recently raised your price.

There are also signs that might encourage you to raise your price:

- You are the only business in the area and your price is no higher than competitors some distance away.
- You have had no complaints about price from your customers.
- You can afford a small drop in demand if you try out a price increase.
- Your product or service is very new and few people offer it.
- Competitors are charging higher prices.
- You have not increased your price in the last year.

A small increase in price, with no fall in demand, can raise your profits substantially and remove the need for cost cutting. Many organisations are afraid to raise prices and resort to cost cutting to remain solvent. Cost cutting is a long, difficult exercise with no guarantee of success – raising prices is simpler, but only if sales will not be affected.

Of course, cutting your prices slightly may increase the demand for your product or service to such an extent that you make considerably more profit. This might be the case if:

- Your price is much higher than competitors and your product or service very similar.
- You can cut your price considerably below your competitors and still make a profit at current sales levels.

A simple guide to raising prices:

- Put your prices up when everyone else does – do not delay.
- Keep price increases modest for any one rise – not a lot more than inflation.
- Do not put prices up too often.
- If you have a large cost increase, explain this to your customer when you raise your price.
- Do not try and put your prices up when others do not unless your price is considerably lower than theirs.
- Try and find somewhere that you can reduce a price when you put others up. This indicates that you are not doing 'across the board' increases.
- Pay particular attention to your major customers – explain things to them, warn them of the increase in advance, perhaps delay their increase for a short time.

THE SALESFORCE

If you already have a salesforce, the first question to ask is – do you need one? What are the alternatives?

- Using agents.
- Using a distributor or wholesaler.
- Telesales yourself, or through a specialist company.
- Direct mail.
- Advertising.

Normally, all the above will be cheaper than your own salesforce but may not do the job as well. The calculation that you need to make is:

Will the savings in cost more than compensate for lost sales?

Of course, if your salesforce is not doing a good job, you may save costs and increase sales as well. If you are exporting, then agents will probably be a better choice than your own salesforce as they will have expert local knowledge.

The first thing that you must do is to calculate the real cost of your salesforce. You should do this by means of writing down all costs as in the chart below.

Salary	National Insurance	Sick pay and holiday costs	Cars, fuel and travel	Hotels and meals	Overheads including admin.	Other

Total up for a total sales cost – and express this as a percentage of turnover. This will give you a 'selling cost percentage' to compare with other methods of selling.

You may decide to keep some of your salesforce in particularly productive areas, and only use an alternative selling method for the balance.

Agents

The best agent is one that chooses you! If you are contacted by an agent then you know that the agent is keen, probably understands your product/service area and wants to work for you. If you have not been contacted by an agent then finding one can be a daunting task. Some methods are:

- Advertising in national newspapers – usually in the small advertisements under 'Agents'.
- Advertising in trade journals.
- For overseas agents, advertising in local papers *in English*. If they do not speak English they are unlikely to be useful unless you speak their language fluently! Sometimes the trade departments of foreign embassies can be useful.
- Taking a stand at a trade fair – as well as customers you will meet agents.
- Looking in trade magazines for agents advertising complimentary rather than competing products/services.

An agent acts as your intermediary with your customer. The agent may act in your name and may be able to negotiate price, depending on the contract. Agents may have a retainer plus commission, or commission only. You will still supply your goods or service direct to the customer. You will have to calculate whether the agent'(s) retainer and commission will be less than the total cost of selling with your own salesforce. You will also have to estimate whether the agent(s) will sell less or more than your own salesforce.

A good agent:

- Does not handle products/services directly competing with you.
- Already visits most of your customers with complimentary products/services.
- Is knowledgeable in your specialist area.
- Gets on well with you and can be trusted by you.

You might want to consider part-time agents if your product or service is suitable. If you are selling direct to individual consumers then the use of part-time agents may be ideal. Many cosmetic, clothing and household goods' companies sell in this way. There is no reason why services such as gardening, window-cleaning and car maintenance should not use the same method. Using your time to provide the service and using a part time agent to find customers may be the most cost-effective way.

Distributors and wholesalers

These sell in their own name, buying your product/service and reselling it. If you have a product, they will usually buy it from you and hold in stock. If you are offering a service, they will pay you for it and recharge their customer. They will either negotiate a price from you, or will agree a discount on the price at which you normally sell.

Distributors and wholesalers are normally well known in your trade, and you will know their reputation. You will have to calculate whether their cost to you compares well with your sales cost and whether they will sell less or more than your own salesforce. Distributors and wholesalers may well be selling products/services which directly compete with yours. You will have to be sure that they will produce the business that you require.

Telesales

Telesales can be very effective and can save considerable amounts on a direct salesforce. They can be used to replace all or part of a salesforce. However, not all products/services are suitable for telesales. A customer is unlikely to buy a 40 ft articulated vehicle worth £40,000 from a telesales call! Telesales are most suitable where:

- You are making a routine call to a customer who places regular orders.
- You know that a potential customer is likely to be buying a particular product or service.
- You know, or can easily find out, who will be responsible for placing the order.
- Your salesforce would be making a lot of exploratory calls in which case an initial telesales call will be very cost effective and can be followed up by someone in person if necessary.
- The likely order is of high enough value to pay for the call. It is not unusual to get an order from 10% of calls. This means that one order must cover the cost of at least ten calls!

Telesales can be operated by an organisation itself, or by a specialist agency. There are three main options:

- Carry out all selling by telesales.
- Use telesales only for specific areas where the salesforce is not cost effective.
- Use telesales to make the initial call to see if there is interest and follow up with a sales representative making a personal call. This can cut sales' costs considerably and is a good way of testing the effect of telesales on your operation.

Often a specialist agency (such as Teleconnexion Telemarketing: see 'Useful Addresses') will be a more cost-effective way of teleselling, but has the disadvantage that the agency may not be as knowledgeable as your own staff. If the telesales operation is to be a large one, then the agency will ensure that its staff are dedicated to your operation and fully knowledgeable. A smaller operation will use agency staff who may be working with several accounts and will not be fully conversant with your product/service unless it is a simple one.

If you decide to use your own staff, then it is essential that they are fully trained in the technique. Suitable courses are available from many training agencies and consultants. It is always possible to use staff for prospecting calls on potential customers when they have a slack period in their normal job. For example, accounts staff may have regular days during the month when they are not working to capacity and could be used (if trained) for this purpose.

You must compare telesales costs with your normal selling costs to make a judgement on whether telesales will cut costs or increase business. Training a member of staff to make prospecting calls on potential customers will be a very cost-effective way of starting.

Direct mail

Direct mail can be a very cost-effective way of selling, but the sales resulting from direct mail are often low compared to telesales. Where telesales can result in 10% of calls being converted to sales, direct mail often has a figure of 1%. This means that it is particularly important to target direct mail at an audience likely to be receptive. This means that direct mail is best:

- For existing and past customers.
- For potential customers that you know use a similar product/service. These are often identified in a trade directory.
- Where a mailing list is available (usually from a specialist agency – for example Keywords Direct: see 'Useful Addresses') for organisations or individuals likely to become customers.
- Where your product/service can easily be described on paper.

Direct mail can cut your costs by finding suitable potential customers for the salesforce to contact. A mailshot enclosing a reply card requesting further information or a personal visit is ideal for this purpose. Direct mail can also be useful for selling direct in areas where your salesforce is not cost effective. It is, however, an expensive medium. Most mailshots to a potential customer group involve thousands of items making a very high cost. You will have to be certain that the mailing will be cost effective. As a rule of thumb assume that 1% of your mailshots result in an order and compare the costs with your existing sales' costs. If you have a very accurate mailing list with only guaranteed potential customers on it, then you may be able to obtain a much higher sales rate than 1%, although a rate in excess of 10% is very unlikely.

The Post Office (Tel: 0345 950950) offers discounts for bulk mailings and there are specialist mailing houses (see *Yellow Pages*) offering a service of producing and mailing out your mailshots.

Remember, *Yellow Pages* can be an effective source of potential customers for Telesales or Direct Mail! Buying a copy of all the *Yellow Pages* for your target area will be much cheaper than buying a mailing list. If your customers can be categorised under *Yellow Pages'* headings then this is almost always the most cost-effective source of contacts.

Advertising

Advertising can cut costs where you have an unidentified group of customers in a geographical area which is unsuitable for your salesforce to visit to establish potential customers. You will not be able to use telesales or direct mail since you have not identified your customers.

The publications in which you intend to advertise should be able to provide a breakdown of their readership to enable you to establish that the publication is suitable for reaching your target market. It usually pays to use an advertising agent (see *Yellow Pages*). The agent will normally be able to negotiate a discount on the advertisement charge that will wholly or partly cover the agency costs. The agent should be able to give you expert advice on the best publications and advertisement format.

A way of cutting costs may be to use PR (public relations) instead of advertising. You can use a PR agency (see *Yellow Pages*) or carry out the work yourself. If you have an innovative or interesting product/service, then you may be able to get editorial coverage in a suitable publication. This is free, so much cheaper than advertising, and people tend to believe an editorial more than an advertisement! Many publications will do a deal. They will give you editorial coverage if you take out an advertisement.

SALES ADMINISTRATION

Often costs can be cut by altering the sales administration process. The first question to ask is:

What are the processes that we use in making a sale? What records do we keep?

In one company that I worked for, the sales team had to fill in a plan for the week, a report form for each visit and a report for the whole week at the end of the week. Each salesperson spent, on average, half a day a week filling in forms! The forms were collated in the sales office and cross-indexed against customers by a sales clerk. I was the sales manager and spent half a day a week studying the plans, call reports and weekly reports. These were summarised in a report for the sales director who spent half a day a week reading my report and writing comments. None of this actually produced any sales, but the total costs were considerable – roughly 10% of our staffing costs!

If you have a paperwork system surrounding your sales, then you can almost certainly save considerable costs by cutting this down. In many cases the system is really to double check on sales representatives' activities. This implies that you cannot trust them! A strange attitude towards key members of staff. You can carry out an audit of this system as follows:

Document	Purpose	Is it essential? Could we do without it?	Could it be combined with another document?	Could it be altered to a simpler format?

Action by rep. or admin.	Purpose	Is it essential? Could we do without it?	Could it be combined with another task?	Could it be made more simple?

In this way you can examine all tasks and paperwork and determine the minimum necessary to carry out the sales function efficiently. In some cases costs can be saved by investing in suitable software so that all sales information is available on a portable computer carried by each representative. The central computer in the sales office can be updated by, and in turn update, the portable computers via one simple phone call each evening.

Sales' costs can also be cut by combining sales enquiries, orders and invoices in one form – either computer generated or a multipart carbonless form. As an example, a phone or mail enquiry can generate a single form which acts as:

- A request for a sales call. There can also be a simple, ticked box report on the call.

- An order form.
- A delivery note.
- An invoice.

This form gives the sales representative the information required to plan visits and report back to the sales office on the visit. It provides an order form which generates a delivery note and enables an invoice to result. Some forms also have a final copy printed up as a payment chaser! This one form could replace an entire sales and accounting document system. Forms such as this can be obtained ready-printed from specialist business stationery suppliers or produced in-house.

MINIMISING COST OF DIRECT SALES

Each area of direct sales' costs needs to be examined:

- Pay versus commission.
- Number of representatives used.
- Sales management structure.
- Costs of transport.
- Costs of accommodation and meals.
- Phone, postage etc ('other').

Pay versus commission

If you could sell more of your product/service then you could well cut costs by increasing sales levels. Increased production or provision of service levels usually results in lower costs per item. If this is the case in your organisation, and you employ your own salesforce, then you should consider introducing a commission on sales over a certain level.

To do this you should calculate the normal sales level for each representative and then offer a percentage commission on all sales over this level. The commission needs to be substantially less than the savings made for the increased sales, but still enough to encourage the representative to make the extra effort to gain the sales.

You might also want to consider the possibility of cutting the number of representatives and offering the others commission on extra sales from the vacated areas. This would mean ensuring that representatives in neighbouring areas could cover the required territories. This makes more effective use of your staffing levels.

Number of representatives used

You should already have produced a chart for analysing total sales costs:

Salary	National Insurance	Sick pay and holiday costs	Cars, fuel and travel	Hotels and meals	Overheads incl. admin.	Other

From this you can extract the relevant direct sales costs for use as follows:

Representative	Area	Customers	Total wage costs	Travel costs	Hotel and meals	Other costs	Total sales

Customer	Sales value	Cost of sales' call*	Area	Frequency of call needed	Actual call frequency	Current representative

* Cost of sales' call calculated by dividing total costs of the representative by the number of calls made by the representative.

A careful study of these two charts will show important facts such as:

- Representatives with particularly high or low total costs.
- Representatives with high or low travel costs.
- Customers with high cost of sales relative to sales value.
- Customers with high or low frequency of calls relative to requirements.

From these facts you should be able to establish:

- The ideal number of representatives.
- The split of customers between representatives that gives each representative the correct number of calls to make, dependent on the area and position of each customer.
- Customers that are not viable on existing cost of sales.
- Representatives that cost too much compared to sales made.

As an aid to this analysis you can use one of the computer programs suitable for route planning, which can give the ideal route for visiting a number of customers, and the total mileage involved (for example, Microsoft AutoRoute Express for under £50).

This exercise will take some time and may require data collection. It can lead to considerable cost savings through reorganisation of representatives and customers. In many cases either fewer representatives can be used, or more customers can be serviced.

Sales management structure

If you have a large salesforce, then it will be essential to have sales management. If you have only a small salesforce, below ten, then any sales management requirement is questionable. It will be more cost effective to have either a senior representative responsible for the salesforce, or to have a 'working' sales manager who is selling full time to customers and has no desk-based function. If you have under ten representatives and have a sales management structure then you should examine the possibility of cutting costs through only having representatives. The senior representative could report direct to the managing director and be given half a day a week for sales administration. Salaries and expenses would be the responsibility of the managing director with the senior representative only responsible for overseeing the salesforce and planning calls. This works well in many companies.

If you have over ten representatives, or a sales manager is essential for other reasons (such as dealing with major customers), then you should examine the existing structure and costs carefully. If you have eliminated much of the paperwork, using the suggestions above, then your sales administration needs will have been reduced. You should consider whether you need the same number of sales administration staff – almost certainly you will not.

Cost of transport

Providing transport for sales representatives can be very expensive. Many sales representatives have their salaries exceeded by travel and other expenses! Cutting down in this area is often more effective than reducing staff levels.

The first area to examine is company cars. Chapter 7 dealt with leasing versus purchase or hire. The questions we need to ask on the sales side are:

- Is it more sensible to allow representatives to buy their own cars and charge mileage? The advantages to the representative are that they can purchase the car of their choice, it is theirs should they leave and they are likely to be able to subsidise some of their private use. If you use a mileage scheme such as allowed by the Inland Revenue, ie approximately 40p per mile for the first 4000 miles, then 20p a mile, you will probably save on the costs of a leased or purchased car.

- Do you need to buy a large car? If they were charging mileage on a private car then many representatives would buy a 'nearly new' or small car to maximise the income from their mileage payments. There is no reason why you should not do the same. Many major manufacturers sell low-mileage, six-month old cars at several thousand pounds off their list price. Ex-hire cars can be bought at auction with less than ten thousand miles and at under six months old. Changing from the top specification to the mid-specification of a model can save several thousand pounds, as can moving to a smaller model.

- If, for prestige reasons, you have to supply a smart top model, then consider selling at around 10,000 miles or one year. If you have bought new at a heavy discount (as you should have done if you are buying numbers of cars) then selling the car early ensures:
  - A good resale value compared with your discounted purchase price.
  - You have spent nothing on spares or servicing. Even breakdowns will normally have been covered under a manufacturer deal with the AA or RAC.
  - Your representative always has the latest model.

- Some companies are now offering a motor bike instead of a car. This is not as strange as it seems. There are the following advantages:
  - Many representatives like the image afforded by a high-quality motor bike. New bike protective gear enables them to still wear a suit! They can buy a cheap car for family use, but many who want a bike will be single.
  - Your company image may benefit from the modern speedy appearance of a salesforce on motor bikes.
  - It costs much less to run a bike than a car.
  - A bike cuts through city traffic in far less time than a car. There may be considerable time (and cost) savings for a city-based representative.

Cost of accommodation and meals

These can be very high for representatives covering a wide area. Meals and accommodation can easily amount to £75–100 a day if hotels from the major groups are used. Cost cutting methods that should be considered are:

- If you decide to continue using major hotel groups, then negotiate a company discount. A 15–25% discount is not unusual.
- Ensure that overnight stays are only authorised when absolutely essential. Often the reorganisation of areas and call cycles can eliminate a lot of overnight stays.
- Consider a subsistence allowance (after discussion with your accountant or the Inland Revenue). Many representatives would prefer an allowance of £40 to spending £75 in a three-star hotel. They will stay in a small, friendly guest house or pub and pocket the difference.
- Enforce a maximum cost that will cover only a small one- or two-star hotel. Often this will be half the cost of a major group and will still offer good standards of comfort.
- Many companies only cover the cost of an evening meal and breakfast, not lunch. In addition they place a strict limit on the cost of a meal.

'Other' expenses

Careful control of phone expenses is essential. Some methods are:

- Representatives can often phone the office in the evening and leave messages on an answer phone rather than phoning during peak hours.
- All representatives should have a phone company credit card which enables them to phone from charge phones at normal rates. It also provides a printout of every call made to ensure that all are on company business. The same card should be used to make calls from home.
- If representatives have portable computers, then these can be linked to the company computer at night and e-mail sent backwards and forwards automatically. This is often cheaper than phoning during the day and sending documents through the post.
- It may be worth while providing representatives with faxes. A couple of pages sent off peak will be cheaper than the post and very much quicker.

DISTRIBUTION

The cost of getting your goods or service to the customer can be very high. If you are providing a service you can often cut costs by subcontracting rather than transporting your own staff where the customer is some distance away. When this is done you will have to build in a method of quality control. As an example, if you service computers for a national company, you may easily be able to provide your own service engineers for most of the areas. There may be some where it is cheaper to subcontract to another service company. You may even be able to make reciprocal arrangements where you service some of their contracts that are nearer to you.

If you are supplying goods then you need to consider the following:

- Do your goods have special transport requirements which mean that it is best to use your own transport? An example might be specially fragile goods that need vehicles with special air suspension.
- Are there special time constraints that mean it is best to use your own transport? An example might be aircraft spares that must reach the customer within a few hours.
- Are there any other reasons that mean that your transport is best?

If you have to use your own transport, then the main methods of cutting costs are by ensuring that routes are scheduled for minimum time and mileage, and that you have no more vehicles and drivers than you need. Route scheduling can be achieved through appropriate software. Vehicle and driver requirements can be calculated by looking at standard delivery patterns. Costs can often be saved by having slightly less vehicles and/or drivers than required for occasional peaks, and hiring in at peak times.

If your goods do not have to be transported by your own vehicles then costs may be significantly cut by contracting your distribution to a specialist company for all or part of your distribution. You may find it most cost effective to deliver within a four-hour drive from your premises (a suitable round trip) and contract out for greater distances. You will need to check that the contractor:

- Will cut costs on your own transport.
- Will be able to handle your particular product.
- Will be able to deliver on time and in the manner required by your customer.
- Will have a suitable image for your company.

Whether using your own or contracted transport, the quantity delivered can greatly affect costs. You may be able to cut costs substantially by offering a discount for greater quantities. For example, if a customer regularly orders half a vehicle load then you would make substantial cost savings by encouraging the customer to order in full vehicle loads. The discount given would have to be less than the cost savings.

For small quantities of goods you should consider Parcel Force for items up to 1.81 kg in weight, and companies such as TNT (Tel: 0800 224466) for items above this weight. Both can guarantee delivery both in the UK and overseas.

SUMMARY

You should regularly check that the prices that you charge for goods or services are suitable. Conditions in the market-place can alter quickly and make your prices out of date. You may be able to raise or lower prices and make a substantial increase in your sales.

Sales and distribution can be very costly. A detailed analysis will enable you to identify areas for substantial cost savings. The analysis will also enable you to identify areas where you can improve your performance and provide a better service to your customers.

You should consider alternatives to running your own sales and distribution. It is often cheaper and more effective to use agents, wholesalers or carriers. It may also cut costs to use telesales or direct mail for all or part of your sales process.

SEVEN

CREATING A COST CONSCIOUS CULTURE

People are naturally resistant to change. They usually prefer the system that they know, the 'tried and tested'. I am sure that you can think of times when you have worried about a change and resisted it! If you make changes in order to achieve cost savings, you are likely to meet resistance. Resistance will probably not be obvious; new systems will take longer than expected to implement, reasons will be found not to implement changes. This is natural!

Every organisation has a 'culture', this is the way things are done, the way people feel and act. It will have evolved during the life of the organisation and will be difficult to change. It will, however, have to be changed if you are to have any chance of your cost cutting programme working. Unless employees themselves understand the need for cost cutting, and are willing to help implement changes, you will have an uphill struggle.

In order to ensure that your cost cutting changes work, and ensure that further cost savings will occur in the future, you will have to:

- Explain the reasons for cost cutting.
- Achieve employee participation in the process.
- Empower employees to suggest, assist and act.
- Identify forces that will resist the process, and remove or weaken them.
- Identify forces that will help the process and strengthen them.
- Appoint groups and individuals that will continue the process.
- Continually communicate with employees.

If you can change your culture to one of cost saving and motivate employees to cut costs, you will have in place a system that will continue to minimise costs and maximise output. This must be one of the most important changes that can take place in any organisation! We will look at each step in turn.

EXPLAINING THE REASONS

If you do not fully explain the reasons for major changes then you are likely to start a rumour factory and a resistance movement! These will both work against you. Fully explaining the reasons for change may not ensure co-operation initially, but is the start of a process that will lead to co-operation. You will need to explain the need for cost cutting and the need for any specific measures that you propose. If people understand your reasons for actions that cut costs, they are more likely to support them and even come up with improvements!

The most suitable methods for explaining will depend on the size and nature of your organisation.

- In a small organisation (under 50 people) the best method may be a personal explanation to individuals or small groups of two or three. Although this may take time it will ensure that employees will feel that they are valued by being given a personal explanation. It will also allow questions to be fully answered.
- In a medium-sized organisation (50–1000 people) group meetings are probably the best method. Use can be made of audio-visual presentation methods to give a full explanation. A suitable period at the end must be devoted to answering all questions as fully as possible. Failure to answer questions honestly will lead to suspicion.
- In a large organisation (over 1000 people) initial details can be given by newsletters, house magazines and videos. It will still be essential to have meetings attended by a senior member of management to deal with any questions that have not been covered by the above methods.

In any explanation it is essential that employees feel that they have been told the truth, told the 'full story' and allowed to ask questions to clarify any points that they did not understand.

ACHIEVING EMPLOYEE PARTICIPATION

If employees can be persuaded to participate in the change process which leads to cost savings, the process is much more likely to be successful. Employees can participate as individuals, as members of a group, or through representatives. The most effective method will be as individuals, the least effective through representatives.

A relatively small change is best handled by individual or group participation. Once the change, the reasons for it and the cost savings likely to result have been fully explained, participation should be sought well *before* any changes are introduced. Employees must feel that their participation can alter the change process if they are to be persuaded to participate. Token participation with no ability to influence is likely to dissuade employees from participation and lead to resistance to the changes.

A large change will take time and the best method of employee participation may be a small group of employees representing total employee views, and reporting back to the rest of the employees.

Remember that employees are likely to be the best resource for planning cost cutting changes and their participation is likely to lead to a smoother change and greater savings.

EMPOWERING EMPLOYEES TO SUGGEST, ASSIST AND ACT

In many organisations the customer is a necessary evil, management criticise freely, employees have little access to information and take no part in decision making. Cost cuts are imposed from above and resisted from below.

In an empowering organisation the customer is king, management freely gives praise, employees have access to information and are involved in decision making. Cost cuts are suggested from below and above.

In an empowering organisation employees (who are often in the best position to see potential savings) are encouraged to make suggestions. There may be formal mechanisms for this, groups' committees, quality circles etc, or simply an atmosphere that encourages suggestions. Where cost savings are to be implemented employees feel able to assist in the process and able to act to ensure that the savings materialise.

In the empowering organisation managers believe that employees are willing and able to suggest methods of cost cutting. They encourage it.

For the concept of the empowering organisation in greater detail I suggest you read *Empowering People* by Jane Smith.

IDENTIFYING FORCES THAT WILL RESIST THE CHANGE

In any situation involving change there will be forces that will help the change and forces that will restrain the change. By identifying these forces you will be able to take action to ensure that the required change happens with the minimum problems.

Where you are making a change that will result in cost cutting, you will inevitably have restraining forces that will hinder the change. Examples are:

- Fear of job losses.
- Fear of extra work.
- Fear of extra controls that will lessen job satisfaction.
- Fear of the unknown.
- Trade union opposition.
- Lack of funds.
- Resistance by managers who think their authority will be undermined.

These are only a few! Such restraining forces can slow down and complicate the change, and delay and lessen the cost cutting. Any steps that can be taken to minimise or remove these restraining forces will obviously result in a more effective change resulting in more effective cost cutting.

Fear of job losses

This is usually the biggest fear in any cost cutting change. Employees who fear that their jobs may be at risk will almost certainly resist the change. If there is no possibility of any job losses, then a guarantee to this effect should be formally made at the earliest possible time. If there are likely to be job losses then this should also be made clear as soon as possible. Certainty is much better than rumour. If the size of job losses is clear, then a statement giving details should be made, including an indication of how they are to be made (early retirement, voluntary redundancy etc).

Co-operation is much more likely if management are seen to be open and honest in this area.

Fear of extra work

Cost cutting changes often make employees work harder. This is not always the case, some changes lessen employees' workload. Most employees, however, see changes as likely to increase their personal workload. For this reason it is essential that all changes are fully discussed with employees as early as possible. The impact on workloads should be specifically addressed and employees allowed to suggest any modifications that will help them without affecting cost savings. They are more likely to accept changes over which they feel that they have had some control.

Where a group of employees has an overall workload they should be allowed to discuss and propose the sharing out of this workload. They will usually do this more effectively than a supervisor or manager!

Fear of extra controls that will lessen job satisfaction

For many employees job satisfaction is an essential element of work. Changes will be seen as threatening job satisfaction. Many employees have 'customised' their jobs to give themselves maximum satisfaction with minimum effort. Any changes will be seen as threatening this situation. It will be necessary to ask whether the changes are likely to affect job satisfaction (the answer will almost certainly be 'yes'!) and if so what could be done to help matters, without affecting cost savings.

Fear of the unknown

This is really the basis of all the above fears. Change is usually feared because the change and its effects are an unknown territory. In order to minimise this fear it is essential to:

- Fully detail the proposed changes as early as possible.
- Indicate the likely effects of the changes.
- Allow discussion by employees.
- Encourage suggestions from employees.
- Give employees as much control over the change as possible.

Trade union opposition

If trade unions are involved in your organisation then they should be involved in receiving information and making suggestions at the same time as the employees. If the majority of the employees are union members then, in general, it will be politically wise to advise the union of the change beforehand. This will ensure that union officials are not caught out by an unexpected announcement of changes. Union officials can be very helpful in explaining changes to employees in a positive manner, but will only do so if you have fully discussed the changes with them beforehand.

Lack of funds

It is often a question of chicken-and-egg! Cost cutting changes often need money initially in order to generate the later cost savings and the initial money is often hard to find. If a change is going to cost money then it is essential to produce a cost-benefit analysis.

A cost-benefit analysis costs each part of the proposed change and shows the benefit in financial or other terms.

Proposed change element	Benefit	Cost/time/labour saving

By breaking down a proposed change in this way, you can ensure that each element of the change is really needed and does produce a worthwhile benefit. In addition such an analysis can be shown to your bank or other finance source to make a case for a loan to cover the change costs until the savings start to accumulate.

Resistance by managers who think their authority will be undermined

Managers often get left out in change plans for cost savings! Employees and unions are consulted but managers, who have the same fears, are ignored. Managers should be informed and consulted in the same way as other employees. In many cases they will need to be consulted before plans are finalised to ensure that there are no unforeseen problems. In particular, managers should be encouraged to discuss any perceived lack of controls in the proposals.

IDENTIFYING FORCES THAT WILL HELP THE PROCESS AND STRENGTHENING THEM

In almost any change there will be forces that help drive the change through. If these can be strengthened then the change will be more likely to be successful. Examples are:

- Survival: the organisation may not survive if costs are not cut.
- Financial: costs may have to be cut to achieve financial targets.
- Jobs: cost cutting may make an organisation more competitive and save jobs.
- People: people (not least yourself!) may support the change and want it to succeed.

If we can build on these forces that drive the change through, and make them stronger, then the change will be easier and more likely to work.

Survival

This is said to be the strongest human instinct! If your organisation's survival is dependent on the proposed changes, and if you explain this fully to employees, you should be able to obtain co-operation. You will need to fully explain the reasons why the organisation will not survive without the changes. This means that you will have to make a presentation to employees which lays out the facts.

If action has to be immediate, this needs to be made clear. Employees have to understand that speedy change is required for survival. Where this is understood, employees will usually be willing to accept autocratic direction on what has to be done, rather than seek a democratic process. In emergencies most people are willing to be told what to do as long as they feel that the person giving the instructions knows what they are doing.

If action does not have to be immediate, then the best results will be obtained by a participative process, allowing the employees to make suggestions and comments.

Financial

Financial reasons are always the most difficult for employees to understand. Your financial constraints and targets may not coincide with what they feel is in their own best interests. It is essential to ensure that your employees realise that your financial targets are in their interests because they will benefit from the resulting stability. If you cannot show this, and employees suspect that changes will only result in increased profits for shareholders or owners with no benefit to themselves, you will have little co-operation.

You will need to present facts that will show benefits to employees in addition to benefits to shareholders or owners. In many cases the simplest way to do this is to ask employees what benefits they would like to see. Often employees' requirements can be fitted in alongside your financial requirements at little or no extra cost. Employee benefits do not have to be financial, there may well be different working practices to give them more satisfaction.

Jobs

Where changes will save jobs, they are likely to be supported by employees if it is the employees' own jobs that are at risk. If the jobs at risk are in another department, then employees are less likely to co-operate.

Where the changes and potential job losses are in the same department, then an explanation of the situation needs to be made, outlining how jobs are at risk, and how the changes will safeguard jobs. Where they are in different departments then a joint meeting should be held, the same explanation given, and discussion between the two departments encouraged. In this way the department being asked to make the changes will be motivated to co-operate by seeing the results of co-operation in the tangible form of other employees' jobs.

People

Where individuals want a change to succeed, for whatever reasons, they will be motivated to try and help the change process as much as possible. Employees may wish the change to succeed for the reasons listed above. Individuals may wish the change to succeed to secure their job, increase their pay, enhance their promotion prospects or increase their power (to name but a few reasons!).

Where individuals will benefit from a change, it is in your interests to ensure that they are aware of this. They will be more likely to co-operate and help the change advance if they are aware of the personal benefits.

For this reason, it is worth while spending time before a change identifying who will benefit from it and then ensuring that they are aware of the facts. This will almost certainly mean a number of individual discussions with key people who can benefit from the change.

APPOINT GROUPS AND INDIVIDUALS THAT WILL CONTINUE THE PROCESS

One of the main problems with most change processes is that once started there is often not enough energy in the organisation to see the change through. Managers often think that if the change process is outlined and started, it will continue through to completion. This is rarely the case.

It will only be possible to ensure the completion of the change process if it has been properly planned and specific provision made for continuing the process through to the end. This will require the setting in place of individuals or groups whose task it is to ensure that the change progresses. In a small organisation this may well be a single individual (often the owner, director or manager). In a larger organisation more elaborate arrangements will be required, usually involving several individuals and/or groups.

The individuals involved, or the members of groups, must be people motivated to see the change succeed. There is little point in entrusting a change process to those who are not keen to see that it succeeds.

Clear targets should be set for the change process with 'milestones' identified to ensure that the process is on track and on time. It is particularly important to identify a method of determining when the change process has finished. Individuals or group(s) should be set up to monitor the progress of the change, ensure that it is progressing as planned and the required outcomes occur. The composition of a group will obviously depend on the particular change, but as a basic principle should include some expertise in the particular area being changed and both management and employee representation, preferably from the area being affected by the change. The individual or group should be required to make progress reports both to management and to the employees affected by the change.

Many organisations bring in an expert change facilitator from outside the organisation to chair the change groups and provide an independent viewpoint. An expert facilitator can ensure that the change is seen as fair and unbiased.

CONTINUALLY COMMUNICATE WITH EMPLOYEES

All too often a change process to achieve reduced costs is started and then the employees are 'forgotten'. If the process is to run smoothly, and if the culture of the organisation is to be changed to one which is cost conscious, then continual communication with employees is essential. Some form of regular progress reporting needs to be established. Where groups have already been set up, as suggested above, to monitor the progress of the change, then these groups can report back to the other employees on a regular basis. An alternative is for the managers concerned to have regular progress meetings with their departments to keep employees informed.

It is particularly important to keep employees informed of cost savings that are made. They need to know that all the upheaval has actually produced results!

GETTING YOUR EMPLOYEES TO SUGGEST COST CUTS

Often the best suggestions for cost cuts will come from your employees. These suggestions are valuable because:

- The employees know the situation better than anyone else and are likely to be able to identify the real areas for cost cutting.
- If employees have suggested the areas for cost cutting, they are likely to be willing to implement their own suggestions!

Employees can be encouraged to suggest cost cuts either through seeing that it is to their long-term advantage to make the organisation more viable (as outlined in the sections above) or through more direct short-term incentives such as offers of cash for suggestions. Beware of offering a percentage of the savings. I was in a company with such a scheme and an employee suggested a major cost savings going into six figures! The company would not pay the 10% they had promised which caused a lot of bad feeling. Either be prepared to pay out several thousand pounds for a brilliant suggestion or offer a maximum sum. Suitable schemes are:

- x% of all savings with a maximum of £xxxx.
- A fixed £xxx for each suggestion implemented.
- A scale of fixed sums depending on the savings achieved.

Some organisations also 'honour' those who have made good suggestions by putting details and a photograph of the employee on their noticeboards. For many people this can be far more important than a cash payment.

Other organisations have found group suggestions to be the most effective. Work groups are encouraged to meet regularly (say monthly) for the specific purpose of suggesting improvements. If their suggestions are accepted, they are then asked to arrange the implementation themselves. There are no specific awards, only praise from management. The group discussions are considered to be part of each employee's job.

PROCESS REENGINEERING

Perhaps the biggest cultural change you can make in your organisation that leads to cost cuts is process reengineering. 'Process' means what 'goes on' in your organisation resulting in a product or service.

The two main methods of achieving cost cuts and performance improvements in the 1990s are continuous process improvement (CPI) and process reengineering. CPI is achieved through the methods outlined earlier in this chapter. It is a continuous process over a period of time. Process reengineering is more radical. Richard Y Chang, in his excellent book *Process Reengineering in Action,* defines it as 'The fundamental rethinking and redesigning of existing process tasks and operating structure to achieve dramatic improvements in process performance'.

Process reengineering involves a complete 'breakthrough' in the organisation's thinking, culture and method of operating. It involves looking at the whole organisation in terms of organisational structure, technology and people. It will involve restructuring, redesigning jobs and examining methods of working. Successful process reengineering can lead to very large cost savings, but it is not easy to implement. Richard Chang's book will guide you through the basic processes, but you may also want to employ a skilled consultant.

SUMMARY

Changing the culture of an organisation takes time and patience. It can take more than a year to start the process of change, but if you are able to achieve a cost conscious culture, it will do more than anything else to reduce your costs.

The secret to creating an effective cost conscious culture is communication. This means communication *from* as well as to your employees. Your employees will often be the best source of cost cutting suggestions and will always be the means of achieving them.

Always try to show that cost cuts are for the employees' benefit as well as the organisation's. You are much more likely to achieve co-operation.

Before implementing cost cutting changes always try to identify forces that will oppose the change and forces that will drive the change through. This identification will enable you to plan implementation of the change with maximum effect. Unplanned change will almost always meet with resistance.

EIGHT

A CHECKLIST FOR COST CUTTING – AN ACTION PLAN

This book can only act as a guide. It can give you ideas and help you think through suitable cost cutting actions. It cannot know your organisation, your employees or you. For this reason you may completely disagree with some of my suggestions, or see ways in which they can be improved. You will also have excellent ideas of your own. You should produce your own personalised cost cutting action plan. Use this checklist only as a means of ensuring that you do not miss anything out.

To produce your plan:

- First of all set a target. What would you like to save – in % or £. This gives you something to aim for. Of course your target must be reasonable!
- Take each department at a time and examine its activities. For each activity ask:
  - What is the activity?
  - By whom is it done?
  - Why is the activity carried out?
  - Does it need to be carried out? Could we do without it?
  - If it has to be carried out, could we do so more cheaply?
- Record each activity and your conclusions.

This is the basis for a cost reduction exercise. It will take time, but it will produce results. The fact that you have examined each activity will enable you to identify areas where costs can be cut. The analysis will enable you to look at the specific areas that we have dealt with in the preceding chapters.

Now, use the checklist to make sure that you have not missed anything out:

50 SPECIFIC CHECK POINTS

Staff

☐ Do we have too many (or too few) levels of management?
☐ Is our structure the best structure for our organisation?
☐ Has each department the ideal number of staff?
☐ Are these staff performing effectively?
☐ Are there any areas where we could contract out?
☐ Are our staff all of the right quality?
☐ Are all jobs structured correctly?
☐ Could we job share or have part-time working to our advantage?
☐ Are our staff fully trained?
☐ Are our staff fully motivated?

Purchasing

☐ Are our purchase decisions reviewed on a regular basis?
☐ Have we someone who understands the basic principles of negotiation?
☐ Do we prepare before our negotiations?
☐ For our major suppliers, are we a valued customer?
☐ Have we identified alternative suppliers for our major purchases?
☐ Have we investigated all aspects of our major purchasing decisions (payment terms, specification, order quantities etc)?
☐ Have we considered whether our suppliers could do some of our work for us?
☐ Are we ordering to suit ourselves or our suppliers?

Finance and stocks

☐ Have we checked our bank charges and taken steps to minimise them?
☐ Have we checked our sources of finance and made sure that they are the most cost effective?
☐ Have we considered whether overdrafts or loans are best?
☐ Have we considered whether to lease, rent or buy?
☐ Have we examined our stocks and identified the most important lines?
☐ Have we taken action to minimise stocks?
☐ Have we instigated a system of debtor control?
☐ Have we discussed maximum payment terms with our creditors?

☐ Have we produced cash flows and a budget system?

Administration

☐ Have we considered how best to utilise our buildings?
☐ Have we considered selling our services to others and buying in rather than providing services?
☐ Have we looked at ways of reducing our post and telephone bills?
☐ Have we considered the alternative methods of providing company cars?
☐ Have we considered the best methods for running company vehicles?
☐ Have we considered savings that could be made on travel and hotels?
☐ Have we considered how we could cut energy and water costs?

IT

☐ Have we looked at our paperwork systems to consider whether they could be computerised?
☐ Have we considered e-mail and the Internet as cost cutting communication methods?
☐ Have we looked at specialist computer programs as a method of saving on staff costs?
☐ Are our staff trained to use computers correctly?

Sales and distribution

☐ Are our prices at the right level?
☐ Have we analysed our salesforce to ensure the right staffing levels?
☐ Have we considered wholesalers and agents as selling methods?
☐ Have we considered telesales and direct mail?
☐ Is our sales administration efficient?
☐ Have we minimised the cost of sales travelling and accommodation?
☐ Have we costed the alternatives of providing our own transport and contracting out?

Culture

☐ Have we enlisted the help of our employees in cost cutting?
☐ Have we empowered employees to suggest, assist and act in cost cutting?
☐ Have we identified the forces that will work against cost cutting changes, and decided how to deal with them?

☐ Have we identified the forces that will help cost cutting changes and strengthened them?

☐ Have we a system for employees suggesting cost cuts?

Your own action checklist of points you have found useful as you read through this book:

☐

☐

☐

☐

☐

☐

☐

☐

☐

☐

☐

- Write down areas that require attention and then list in order of priority.
- Who is going to act on these points? Will you be able to do it all yourself, or will you need to appoint a person or team to do it?
- Have you a time-scale for achieving these cost cuts?
- How will you know when you have succeeded? Have you a financial system in place that will identify the cost savings that you have made?
- What are you going to do with the money that you have saved!

Your help will be valuable!

I am sure that you will have some excellent ideas for cutting costs that I have overlooked! I would be very grateful to hear about these and very pleased to have any comments on this book. Your help will make the next edition even more useful!

You can write to me at the following address:

John Allan
PO Box 178
Tring
HP23 5LS

I cannot promise to answer all letters, but I can promise to read them all with great care.

BIBLIOGRAPHY

Allan, J. (1996) *How to Be Better at Motivating People,* Kogan Page, London.

Barrow, C. (1995) *Financial Management for the Small Business,* Kogan Page, London.

Chang, R. Y. (1996) *Process Reengineering in Action,* Kogan Page, London.

Department of Employment *Procedure for Handling Redundancies.*

Department of Employment *Unfairly Dismissed?*

Department of Trade and Industry *The Regional Initiative – Guide to Regional Selective Assistance.*

Eales-White, R. (1996) *How to Be a Better Teambuilder,* Kogan Page, London.

Fisher, M. (1996) *Performance Appraisals,* Kogan Page, London.

Harrison, J. (1989) *Finance for the Non-financial Manager,* Thorsons, London.

Maddux, R. B. (1988) *Effective Performance Appraisals,* Kogan Page, London.

Maddux, R. B. (1994) *Team Building: An Exercise in Leadership,* Kogan Page, London.

Moon, P. (forthcoming, July 1997) *Appraising Your Staff,* Kogan Page, London.

National Academy of Public Administration *Guide to Responsible Restructuring,* University of Colorado, USA.

Schofield, S. (1994) *The UK Internet Book,* Addison-Wesley, Wokingham.

Smith, J. (1996) *Empowering People,* Kogan Page, London.

USEFUL ADDRESSES

ABB Building Service Ltd
6 & 7 Waltham Park Way
Billet Road
London E17 5DU
Tel: 0181 527 8515

British Venture Capital Association
Essex House
12–13 Essex Street
London WC2R 3AA
Tel: 0171 240 3846

CompuServe
PO Box 676
Bristol BS99 1YN
Tel: 0800 000 200

Cooper Cleaning Ltd
Unit 1
The Chase
John Tate Road
Foxholes Business Park
Hertford SG13 7NN
Tel: 01992 503909

Department of Trade and Industry
1 Victoria Street
London SW1H 0ET
Tel: 0171 215 5000

Dun and Bradstreet
Holmer Farm Way
High Wycombe
Bucks
Tel: 01494 422000

Hi-Grade
43 Thames Road
Barking
Essex IG11 0HQ
Tel: 0181 532 6166

Keywords Direct
Unit 4
Stanton Industrial Estate
Stanton Road
Southampton
Hants SO7 4XA
Tel: 01703 787509

Learning Tree International
Mole Business Park
Leatherhead
Surrey KT22 7AD
Tel: 01372 364610

Local Investment Networking Company Limited
London Enterprise Agency
4 Snow Hill
London EC1A 2BS
Tel: 0171 236 3000

Mortgages for Business
2 East Point
High Street
Seal
Sevenoaks
Kent TN15 0EG
Tel: 01732 763660

Opus Technology PLC
Redhill Business Park
Redhill
Surrey RH1 5YB
Tel: 01293 821555

Pegasus Software Ltd
FREEPOST NH 4169
Kettering
Northants. NN15 6BR
Tel: 01536 495000

Software Warehouse PLC
6 Roman Way
Coleshill Industrial Estate
Coleshill
Warwicks. B46 1HG
Tel: 01675 468330

Tarmac Servicemaster Ltd
37/39 Kew Foot Road
Richmond
Surrey TW9 2SS
Tel: 0181 332 0233

Teleconnexion Telemarketing
135 The Parade
Watford
Herts
Tel: 0181 255 509

3i
91 Waterloo Road
London SE1 8XP
Tel: 0171 928 3131

INDEX